INTRACO

Blazing a Trail Overseas for Singapore?

INTRACO

Blazing a Trail Overseas for Singapore?

Faizal Bin Yahya

Institute of Policy Studies, Singapore

Institute of Policy Studies

World Scientific

Published by

World Scientific Publishing Co. Pte. Ltd.
5 Toh Tuck Link, Singapore 596224
USA office: 27 Warren Street, Suite 401-402, Hackensack, NJ 07601
UK office: 57 Shelton Street, Covent Garden, London WC2H 9HE

British Library Cataloguing-in-Publication Data
A catalogue record for this book is available from the British Library.

INTRACO
Blazing a Trail Overseas for Singapore?

ISBN 978-981-4656-81-8
ISBN 978-981-4623-86-5 (pbk)

In-house Editor: Sandhya Venkatesh

Typeset by Stallion Press
Email: enquiries@stallionpress.com

Printed in Singapore

ACKNOWLEDGEMENTS

This book would not have been possible without the encouragement of Ambassador at Large Ong Keng Yong who was formerly Director of the Institute of Policy Studies and currently the Executive Deputy Chairman of S. Rajaratnam School of International Studies (RSIS), Singapore. Succeeding IPS Director Janadas Devan has also showed great commitment to this book project and it was with much relief that the writer was able to deliver the full manuscript within the time frame required.

Why INTRACO? International Trading Company (INTRACO) was an iconic government-linked company (GLC) in the 1970s and 1980s. It was a byword for adventure and can do spirit for Singapore's bureaucrats turned entrepreneurs and spawned several successful Singaporean entrepreneurial enterprises. The writer wishes to thank the distinguished cast of former INTRACO employees including its chairmen and directors Ang Kong Hua, S. Chandra Das, Ngiam Tong Dow, P. Y. Hwang, David Ho, Gopinath Pillai, Lam Peck Heng, S. C. Tien, Bernard Chen, Seah Chong Leng, Sebastian Yong, Walter Woon, Patrick Yeo, Peter Loh, Tit Yin Seng, Maisie Koh, Latiff, Sam Chong Keen, Thang Kwek Min, Teo Meng Toon, Tan Puay Chuan and Nancy Ng for their time and willingness to share stories and information about INTRACO.

The writer would also like to thank INTRACO's representatives in its present form which is part of the PSC Corporation for sharing its Annual Reports and Newsletters and these were invaluable in piecing together the story of this remarkable former Singapore GLC.

On a personal note, the writer would like to thank his wife Rita and their children Aiman, Nina, Ezra and Ezriel for their love, understanding and patience during the research, writing and publication of this manuscript. Last but not least, the writer wishes to thank Sarjune Ibrahim and Chang Zhi Yang for their assistance in reading various drafts and internal editorial work for this manuscript.

CONTENTS

LIST OF FIGURES

LIST OF PICTURES

LIST OF TABLES

CHAPTER 1

INTRACO AND ITS ROLE IN THE ECONOMIC DEVELOPMENT OF SINGAPORE

INTRODUCTION

Following Singapore's separation from Malaysia in 1965, one of the key challenges for the government was to transform the economy from a re-export model under the colonial regime to that of an export economy. Severed from its natural economic hinterland in Malaysia, Singapore had to trade and expand linkages with the global economy to ensure its survival. Due to a lack of trusted entrepreneurs and financial capital in sectors where risks are great and the returns uncertain, the state created state-owned enterprises, more commonly referred to as government-linked companies (GLCs), to tackle this issue. The objectives of these companies were to assist in the expansion and nurturing of these critical sectors of the economy, including transportation, electricity generation and housing.

At that point in time, very few Singapore companies managed to venture onto the international market due to lack of international networks, financial resources and experience. The splintering of Europe into the Communist East and Democratic West compounded Singapore's minimal political contact with communist regimes as the former had waged an internal war against the Communists during the Malayan Emergency from 1948 to 1960 (Karl, 2009). At the time, the whole of the Southeast Asian region was under the threat of communist insurgency and China was supporting the export of communism and undermining neighbouring regimes.

In addition, when it had become clear in the late 1950s that the British colonial regime was going to leave Singapore, the communists planned to seize control of an independent government by legal means through the ballot boxes as well as continuing to foster civil unrest and disobedience. These were carried out by students, mainly those in the Chinese-medium schools and working-class labourers. In October 1956, after more rioting by students and labourers, Singapore police raided labour unions and schools and rounded up large numbers of communist party members and their supporters.

Despite this, the founding organisers of the People's Action Party (PAP) had also deliberately collaborated with the communists in order to broaden the PAP's organisational base among the Chinese majority. In turn, the communists saw in the leftist orientation of the PAP an ideologically acceptable basis for an alliance. The concurrent effort by the communists to find a legal route to power focused on the party's alliance with the PAP. This strategic political move by the PAP proved to be a double-edged sword when the communists attempted to seize control of the PAP Central Executive Committee in 1957. However, they were defeated by supporters of the PAP and Lee Kuan Yew, both of whom went on to lead the PAP to victory in the 1959 election. As prime minister, Lee gradually eliminated communists from influential positions within the party and government, and later used provisions of the Internal Security Act (ISA) to prevent alleged communists from participating in politics (Baker, 2000, p. 282).

The distrust the PAP had of the communists prevented Singapore from establishing any political or diplomatic links with China and other socialist states. Thereafter, Singapore only established limited political and diplomatic ties with some communist or socialist countries. Yet, as a maritime trading nation whose main economic activity at the time was entrepôt trade, Singapore was pragmatic in its approach to find an avenue to continue trading with communist regimes, especially China. How did the Singapore government device a framework to continue trade and economic links with communist regimes?

This book argues that the Singapore government created GLCs to fulfil strategic economic and political objectives. The objective of this book is to provide an economic narrative of Singapore's development.

The framework of analysis involves examining the various actors and institutions which designed and implemented Singapore's economic blueprint. The book will use a former GLC called International Trading Company (INTRACO) as a case study, situate the company in Singapore's economic history and explain the role that it played in the development of the economy, both as the main vehicle to trade with socialist countries and as a state trading enterprise to fulfil specific strategic objectives such as the creation of a rice stock pile.

With the creation of a strategic rice stock pile and greater economic linkages between Singapore and communist regimes such as China, GLCs like INTRACO may be bereft of their usefulness. The book goes on to examine whether the trading sector has outlived its usefulness or remains a strategic concern for the state. In order to examine this, the book will highlight the role of Temasek Private Limited, a state holding company. Why Temasek? Temasek Private Limited as a holding company was formed to manage the government's shares in the various GLCs. As the holding company that owns the government's shares in most GLCs, it became the responsibility of Temasek Holdings to assist GLCs under its charge to engage in internationally competitive businesses.

As GLCs grew in stature and competitiveness, the public, especially the investors, were keen to know more about the government's policy on divesting its shares in GLCs. However, for strategic reasons where the activities of the GLCs were crucial to Singapore for strategic complementarity, such as aviation connectivity and electricity supply, the government intended to retain its majority or significant stakes in specific GLCs. For the strategic activities that were still wholly-owned, the government intended to eventually list them in order to assist these companies to grow and increase shareholder value. With greater global economic competition, the GLCs were expected to continually enhance their core competencies. For GLCs that had global and regional potential, Temasek intended to grow them to benefit Singapore over the long term. In the event that a GLC was growing into a major player that required the government to dilute its stake through new share issues or mergers or acquisitions, the government was prepared to do so. GLCs that were no longer deemed relevant to the government or Temasek's objectives would be divested by having its shareholdings sold off in a controlled manner.

Temasek's role was also pivotal in the fate of GLCs such as INTRACO as it became the key instrument of divesting GLCs as part of the government's strategic economic planning. This book will argue that while INTRACO did face difficulties fulfilling its key role as the Cold War ended and the global economy became more integrated, nonetheless, it will disagree with categorising INTRACO as a non-core or non-strategic GLC. This book contends that trading remains a strategic interest for the state.

The book will use the context of change model to illustrate those internal influences such as management, staff turnover and strategic planning contributing to INTRACO's failings and subsequent demise. In addition, external changes such as the transformation of the global economy had undermined INTRACO's key strengths as a trading monopoly with communist regimes. Another external key issue is the state itself and the role of Temasek Holdings in INTRACO's demise. The book contends that Temasek's role as the key divestment tool of the government in 1985 had undermined state's support for INTRACO by placing the GLC in the non-core strategic category. Moreover, despite Temasek publishing its charter in 2002 listing one of its objectives to "build and nurture internationally competitive businesses", it also developed its private equity and hedge fund arm at the same time (Temasek Charter, 2002). In this regard, Temasek's role as a private equity or hedge fund would appear to contradict its ability and objectives to develop and nurture Singapore companies. This is because Temasek's role has been transformed from a stakeholder mentality to nurture Singapore companies into a shareholder mentality that is more profit driven. In a shareholder capitalist model, companies should be divested if they are unprofitable and if they continually show losses such as INTRACO. In 2003, INTRACO was fully divested and sold to PSC Corporation.

This book is about the "failure" of a GLC called INTRACO to blaze its own trail overseas. Set against the background of several Singapore GLCs' success stories, it is a reminder that the Singapore government through its brand of state-guided capitalism could also ruthlessly dispense with underperforming GLCs and create alternatives.

At the onset of its economic development, apart from political constraints, Singapore also faced considerable obstacles such as a dearth of entrepreneurial talent. Arguably, as a trading nation, it would be fair to say that Singapore was not short of traders or businessmen. However, from the government's point of view, these traders were mainly seen as rogue profiteers and not to be entrusted with million dollar state projects and the management of GLCs. If the private sector was not to be trusted, where could the government draw the talent to develop the Singapore economy? In addition, Singapore was operating in hostile surroundings, where regional countries were inclined to impose trade restrictions as protectionist measures with Singapore because they too were developing their own fledgling economies. This meant that Singapore's development strategy had to look beyond the region for its markets (Abeysinghe, 2007).

In the early turbulent years of Singapore's independence, one of its main pioneers and architects was Dr Goh Keng Swee, who was the Finance and Deputy Prime Minister from the 1960s to the 1980s. Dr Goh at the very beginning highlighted the critical role of the state in economic development. He said that "the role of government is pivotal [and that] non-economic factors, which have yet to be reduced to a coherent multi-disciplinary system, are more important than economic variables" (Abeysinghe, 2007, p. 2). With national survival in mind, the government actively intervened in the development of the economy and established state-owned enterprises, more commonly known as government-linked companies, or GLCs, in Singapore.

It was fortuitous for Singapore that prior to its separation from Malaysia in August 1965, the Singapore government had established the Economic Development Board (EDB) in 1961. When the EDB was established, one of its key roles was to create employment and boost the national income (*The Straits Times*, 4 April 1961, p. 5). At the time, the strategic economic plan to be implemented by the EDB was to inject S$871 million to develop the industrial sector in Singapore. Why the urgency to develop the industrial sector? The pressure of employment creation was great because between 1946 and 1957, Singapore had the highest rate of population growth in the world at 4.3%. Singapore's population growth combined with a migratory surplus of 75,000 people from the Malaysian Federation between 1948 and 1959 added to the unemployment problem in Singapore.

How critical was employment creation? A projected 78,000 jobs had to be created in 1970 for full employment to be realised in Singapore

(EDB, 1963, p. 2). In this context, industrialisation was seen as a panacea for unemployment and a key tool for employment creation (*The Straits Times*, 17 August 1961, p. 1). In order to accomplish this task, the government granted the EDB an initial capital fund of $40 million (EDB, 1962, p. 2). Manufacturing was a vital component of the economy with the potential to create employment opportunities and a skilled work force. Employment creation was vital and a pressing problem in addition to critical issues such as health, education and housing (*The Straits Times*, 8 April 1968, p. 6).

The EDB's initial task was to develop a framework for Singapore's industrialisation strategy (Singapore Economic Development Board (SEDB), 2011, p. 11). What was the EDB's strategy in expanding industrialisation? The EDB assisted private industry in promoting industrial expansion through the provision of expert personnel, financing and sharing of market research results with local manufacturers (*The Straits Times*, 17 August 1961, p. 6). The EDB also had the authority to grant incentives, establish industrial estates, and it invested directly in new and expanding enterprises (Van Elkan, 1995, p. 12). How did Dr Goh Keng Swee and the EDB inspire investors' confidence in the Singapore economy? Dr Goh had set himself the task of inspiring confidence in Singapore's industries by generating good publicity through officiating at the openings of factory premises. Chan Chin Bock, who was to become EDB's chairman, recalled that his first assignment from Dr Goh in 1964 was to organise a factory opening ceremony every day for three months (Chan, 2002, p. 34). Besides this, there were other events which garnered publicity and highlighted investors' commitment to the projects such as the foundation stone laying ceremony to mark the start of building factories (Chan, 2002, p. 34). This was done even for the smallest factories, like one making mothballs (Lee, 2000, p. 80).

In order to stimulate investment in the economy, the EDB's Investment Promotion Division (IPD) encouraged the private sector to establish new industries or to expand existing plants (EDB, 1963, p. 11). EDB's Projects Division was responsible for identifying industries suitable for establishment in Singapore, and for providing information to investors as well as assisting them with their queries. In the late 1960s, Dr Goh was concerned that from the government's point of view, the EDB had become too big and unwieldy to manage and may lose its focus, which was to attract foreign companies to invest and establish operations in Singapore. In this regard, while other EDB divisions, such as Finance Division, played specific roles in expanding the industrial sector, they too were eventually separated from the EDB and privatised to form GLCs.

The Finance Division was responsible for loan negotiations involving financial analysis and assessments of the credit worthiness of company applications, and for the disbursement and recovery of loans granted by the Board (EDB, 1963, p. 16). In 1962, an estimated $19.7 million was disbursed or committed in the way of loans and equity subscriptions (EDB, 1963, p. 7). In 1968, EDB's Finance Division was eventually privatised as the Development Bank of Singapore (DBS) (Parliamentary Debates Singapore, 1968). Other divisions such as the EDB's Technical Consultant Services Division provided technical consulting services to the industry, while the Industrial Facilities Division was concerned with managing suitable areas for development and industrial estates (EDB, 1963, p. 21). The Industrial Facilities Division was heavily involved in the development of Jurong industrial estate, and then Jurong New Town, a self-contained industrial estate that would serve as the forerunner of Singapore's push for industrialisation (*The Straits Times*, 14 September 1968, p. 5). This Division would eventually become the Jurong Town Corporation (JTC) (Jurong Town Corporation 1969). In the fifth decade since its establishment in 1961, the present-day EDB has a recognised role in attracting investments, developing and enhancing of business environments, as well as catering to the specialised needs of niche markets (EDB, website).

With regards to economic planning, after Singapore's separation from Malaysia in 1965, the EDB had a readily available pool of talented individuals who could spearhead development in relevant sectors. Under Dr Goh's instructions, senior civil servants Sim Kee Boon and Ngiam Tong Dow were both seconded to INTRACO. Sim Kee Boon was appointed the founding Chairman and Chairman of INTRACO's Executive Committee while Ngiam Tong Dow became the Executive Director. A senior EDB officer named Chandra Das who became the Director of the Export Promotion Centre (EPC) under the purview of the EDB was also seconded to INTRACO.

Singapore as a late industrialising nation created GLCs and statutory boards to spearhead development in various sectors of its economy in order to jump-start economic growth. GLCs were companies in which some of the shares were owned by the government. They were subjected to the same regulations and market forces as private entrepreneurs and did not receive subsidies or preferential treatment from the government. INTRACO as a GLC was poised to play a key role in Singapore's economic expansion.

STATEMENT OF PROBLEM

The Singapore government had created GLCs to expand economic growth and development. One of the critical concerns was to connect and strengthen Singapore's business and trade links with the international economy. In this regard, a GLC called INTRACO was established to enhance Singapore's ties with the global economic community. Primarily, its purpose was to navigate through obstacles and circumvent political "road blocks" in order to trade with communist regimes in the Socialist Bloc during the Cold War. INTRACO assumed the role of Singapore's premier state trading enterprise and acted as an intermediary trader between Singapore and the global economic community, especially the Socialist Bloc. The group of countries in the former Soviet Bloc included Bulgaria, Czechoslovakia, East Germany, Hungary, Poland, Romania and the Soviet Union.

In assessing various state-owned enterprises around the world that INTRACO could use as a model and derive lessons for its own development, Japan's general trading companies (GTCs) — more commonly known as *sogo shosha* — stood out. While it could be argued that the pioneer management team at INTRACO did try to emulate *sogo shosha*, INTRACO was not able to achieve its potential and was deemed a failure by its critics in later years.

The need for government intervention in the economy was also crucial because the market did not have the necessary funding to undertake projects deemed necessary for economic development, where the returns on investments were lower and would take a longer time. Moreover, the market did not possess adequate human capital to create an entrepreneurial class to drive the Singapore economy. Hence, civil servants were recruited to staff GLCs such as INTRACO. It will be shown in later chapters that state intervention worked both ways because it facilitated as well as hampered the growth of GLCs such as INTRACO.

Ultimately, the role of the trading company as a "middleman" or intermediary is transitory in nature; even in the 1960s, a few Singapore companies had ventured overseas in search of business and trade opportunities. This trend increased with the government's call for local companies to regionalise and venture overseas in the 1980s. Furthermore, with the changing geopolitical scenario in the global economy — due to the end of the Cold War and increasing economic integration through greater transboundary trade and investments — venturing abroad has become a facet of a globalised world.

The changing global geopolitical context had great influence on the business and trading regimes and networks of Singapore companies. The disintegration of the Soviet Bloc towards the end of the 1980s, the liberalisation of socialist economies such as China and the proliferation of regional trading arrangements and free trade agreements had eroded the exclusive role of INTRACO as a state trading enterprise and intermediary between Singapore and the socialist states.

Were changing global geopolitical conditions the only reasons for INTRACO's demise? The ability of Japan's *sogo shosha* to survive and grow despite the changing global political scenario suggests that INTRACO could have similarly undertaken the same path. The *sogo shoshas* were able to expand beyond their middleman role in the Japanese economy. This indicated that other factors could have contributed to INTRACO's inability to survive and thrive. These factors could include the dynamics between GLCs and the state in relation to the vision and management of GLCs.

METHODOLOGY

In researching for this publication, I visited the current premises of INTRACO to gather an update about the company. I was informed that almost all of INTRACO's archival files that did not pertain to its financial accounts had been destroyed when the lease to INTRACO's warehouse along the West Coast expired in 2008. The only records available were its annual reports and newsletters from 1982 to 1999. I also gathered data from consultancy reports and Parliamentary speeches on INTRACO from the libraries at the National University of Singapore.

INTRACO's annual reports were gathered from 1969 until its complete divestment as a GLC in 2003. Apart from the reports, I also collected copies of INTRACO's now defunct newsletter to gather some insights into the company's corporate culture through the activities and initiatives it implemented.

More than 25 in-depth interviews were conducted with former INTRACO employees. These included 19 interviews with former chairmen, board directors, managing directors, general managers and line managers who served across a span of time, from INTRACO's establishment in 1968 to its divestment as a GLC at the end of 2003. In references to interviews conducted with former senior executives of INTRACO, their anonymity will be maintained by not mentioning their names and through the use of indexed initials.

OUTLINE OF CHAPTERS

The organisation of the book is as follows:

Chapter 1: INTRACO and its Role in the Economic Development of Singapore

The introductory chapter will provide a brief history of INTRACO's establishment, situate the company in Singapore's economic history and explain the role that it played in the development of the economy, especially as the premier state trading enterprise. The chapter will also explain the economic options available for newly independent Singapore in 1965, which faced a number of critical challenges. One of the key challenges was to expand economic growth and development after separating from Malaysia and being disconnected from its natural economic hinterland. In November 1968, INTRACO was created to establish trade and economic linkages with communist countries such as China.

This chapter will also provide the methodological framework and chapter outline of the book. In addition, the chapter will provide the rationale of the scholarly contribution of the book towards understanding the role of state-owned enterprises or GLCs in economic development.

Chapter 2: Singapore's *Sogo Shosha*?

INTRACO as a state trading enterprise was loosely modelled after the famed *sogo shosha* or GTCs in Japan. This chapter will undertake a literature review about state-owned enterprises or GLCs and the *sogo shoshas*. The ability of *sogo shoshas* to survive and expand into various sectors despite the vagaries in the global economy raised the question as to whether the business model that INTRACO had emulated was workable and whether other factors caused its demise. The apparent inability of INTRACO to realign its business strategy in a changing global economy and to expand into new areas suggests internal constraints. These could be due to human capital issues, leadership, company vision and inability to decipher the tacit instructions and advice from the Board.

Chapter 3: State-guided Capitalism

This chapter will examine further the rationale behind the formation of GLCs. The GLCs were managed by bureaucrats-turned-entrepreneurs and this chapter will explain the role of bureaucrats in economic development as part of the state-guided capitalism model which drives Singapore incorporated (Singapore Inc.). Chapter 3 will use INTRACO as a case study and show that the GLC was subjected to internal and external influences as can be seen under the 'Context of Change' model. The chapter will highlight the role played by one of Singapore's Sovereign Wealth Fund (SWF) Temasek Holdings in the development of GLCs such as INTRACO. Moreover, the chapter explains the structure of GLCs such as linkages to Temasek and cross-cutting ownership shares among the various GLCs. The chapter initiates the discussion that contradictions abound as to the continued relevance of INTRACO especially as the global economy changes in a post-Cold War era.

Chapter 4: Strategic Planning — "National Service" — 1960s to 1980

INTRACO's founding chairman Sim Kee Boon developed INTRACO's role as the state trading company and had INTRACO listed on the stock exchange in 1972. This was to enable INTRACO to raise capital for its expansion but it also made the GLC answerable to shareholders. INTRACO also undertook strategic tasks given by the government. One of these was to establish a rice stockpile for Singapore to reduce price fluctuations for this basic commodity. In this regard, INTRACO was also an instrument used by the government to mitigate potentially adverse social impacts caused by shortages in the supply of rice or steep increases in its prices. In addition, as a bulk procurer of raw materials for Singapore companies, INTRACO played its part in contributing to their competitiveness and in exploring new markets for Singapore's exports such as Bangladesh, Sri Lanka, Vietnam and North Korea. In its role to diversify procurement of raw materials from new sources and demand from emerging markets, the government had also given INTRACO the permission to explore and enhance trade with China.

Chapter 5: Internationalisation and "Rough Waters" — 1980s to 1990

The chapter examines the core areas of INTRACO's business activities such as infrastructure development and commodities trading and diversification into new business ventures by acquisitions. Global events had also influenced INTRACO's role and impacted its businesses, and these included: the end of the Cold War in 1989, Singapore's diplomatic outreach to China in early 1990s, the eruption of the First Gulf War in early 1990s with the invasion of Kuwait by Iraq and the culmination of the Yugoslav Wars in late 1990s.

How did the leaders at INTRACO navigate through the turbulent economic conditions and how did they fare? What were the lessons learnt? INTRACO also adopted a "country approach" for its trading business. How effective was this for its operations and profits? Joint ventures with companies like Informatics were made to venture into new markets. INTRACO had also explored business opportunities in exotic locations like Africa, such as the diamond mines of Angola. Some of the areas of INTRACO's business interests during this period included equipment procurement and contract administration, while its other business interests included power supply generation, transmission and distribution equipment. Some of its loss-making ventures included its car dealerships (including brands like Holden, Lada and Rover), commodities' trading and business links with Teledata. INTRACO also continued to explore opportunities in new emerging markets like Myanmar and Vietnam.

Chapter 6: Post-Cold War and Globalisation — 1990 to 2000

The new millennium triggered a wave of mergers and acquisitions. Domestically, in June 2000, the Monetary Authority of Singapore announced a three-year deadline for local banks to dispose of their non-core assets and that GLCs were to follow suit. There was also growing debate about the role of GLCs in Singapore; GLCs were accused of "crowding out" competition from the small and medium enterprises (SMEs) and critics thought the former should venture overseas to create an external economic wing for the country. The stock exchange was also dominated by GLCs, and this had to change if more listings from foreign companies were to be realised. INTRACO's links to its joint ventures were increasingly called into question by local traders. Members of Parliament also debated the role of GLCs and their "crowding out" of local SMEs in the domestic economy. Since INTRACO's original role was to "blaze a trail" overseas, it came under increasing scrutiny by the local trading community. The end of the Cold War effectively ended INTRACO's dominance in trading with socialist economies and the company had to reinvent itself and search for new areas for business opportunities.

Chapter 7: Devolving a Government-linked Company — 2000 to 2003

The chapter examines the "sale" of INTRACO as a GLC. Did it outlive its usefulness and fail to reinvent itself? Did it become too diverse and unwieldy and fail to expand its profits base? The divestments of non-core assets and businesses such as disposal of portfolio investments in shares of DBS Group Holdings consigned INTRACO to being labelled as "non-strategic". In addition, INTRACO was increasingly seen as a liability as it raked several losses and lost its focus — ironically, because of the divestment of its non-core assets and enhancement of its core assets. The bureaucrat entrepreneurs involved in INTRACO then wondered what the company's strategic value was. It became a challenge to keep INTRACO relevant through value-added products and services. The implementation of the INTRACO Enterprise Hub (IEH) concept also proved "too little, too late" for the company. The situation became desperate for INTRACO to reinvent itself when the company ceased to be a Temasek-linked company in late 2003. However, there were some lingering linkages with the state since INTRACO was part of Senior Minister Goh Chok Tong and the Singapore Business Federation's delegation to Tunisia in 2006. INTRACO continues to explore business opportunities in the Middle East. Apart from the Middle East, INTRACO had also enhanced linkages with companies in China; for example, in building agricultural and seafood businesses.

Chapter 8: Conclusion

INTRACO was established to trade and explore business opportunities in closed markets such as socialist economies or emerging markets such as the Middle East or Africa. In certain respects, INTRACO was ahead of the curve in forging business links with international markets. However, INTRACO has seen its role diminish over time and failed to reinvent itself. What were the reasons for this? What were the lessons drawn about the links between the state and the market? The concluding chapter examines the various factors that influenced the development of INTRACO against a backdrop of changing global economic conditions — where geopolitics was at the core of tectonic shifts after the Cold War, and political changes such as the end of the apartheid era in South Africa. The chapter will discuss the relevance and strategic role of trading in Singapore's economic development.

CHAPTER 2

GOVERNMENT-LINKED COMPANIES AND *SOGO SHOSHAS*

MODEL FOR INTRACO?

When INTRACO was established in 1968, the *sogo shoshas* was its model of inspiration. *Sogo shosha* is a term applied to Japan's general trading companies (GTCs) and they are characterised by colossal sales turnover, diversity of goods traded and global reach of their business networks (Tanaka, 2008, p. 172). The Japanese GTCs were established around 1868 when Japan resumed its commercial transactions with the world after a period of self-imposed isolation. GTCs were modelled on similar companies overseas such as the British East India Company or Jardine Matheson (Larke and Davies, 2007). In the early part of Japan's history, as it opened up to global trade, the GTCs were called Zaibatsu — literally, "financial cliques", referring to financial business and industrial conglomerates — and they became significant industrial groupings and major financial institutions with both commercial and political reach throughout the Japanese economy that controlled Japan's international trade.

How did the *sogo shosha* reconnect Japan to the global economy after centuries of isolation? They helped the Japanese economy overcome its constraints of inefficient language skills and lack of familiarity with international trading practices. While it was acknowledged that Japan would not be able to reduce its economic handicaps overnight, it was planning to improve its trading competitiveness by concentrating trading functions into a limited number of specialised companies.

What were the unique qualities of Japanese *sogo shosha* that set them apart from other state-owned enterprises? Some observers pointed out that the *sogo shosha* provided numerous functions that were closely related and difficult to separate. Moreover, they did not have a static set of functions and were able to evolve and develop new functions to respond to the requirements of the global economy (Abe, Mitsui & Co. Ltd). This seemingly unrelated and unwieldy structure of the *sogo shosha* had accorded them strong influence on state matters.

After Japan's defeat in World War II, the Zaibatsu that included *sogo shosha* were dissolved by the Allied forces. Strategic military thinkers argued that the Zaibatsu was one of the key components of the Japanese war machine and to disband it, would be to cripple the expansionist ambitions of future militarist leaders. Therefore, the *sogo shoshas* were separated into different parts. For example, Mitsui Bussan was divided into 200 separate companies and Mitsubishi into 139 — but this fragmentation only lasted as long as the American occupation. Thereafter, from 1952 onwards when the Allied occupation ended, with the same senior managers in place, the fragmented groups quickly moved to rebuild their former position and reconsolidate their economic strengths (Larke and Davies, 2007). However, apart from the *sogo shosha*, well-known Japanese companies such as Toyota, Sony and Honda also began developing as export-oriented companies, which curtailed the *shosha*'s influence. In this context, apart from some key areas like commodity imports, the *sogo shoshas* have not been able to re-establish their dominant monopolistic position in the post-war era. After World War II, the *sogo shosha* were also restricted in some countries such as China to trading with state-owned enterprises and were only allowed to import finished goods such as machinery and equipment from Japan.

As mentioned in Chapter 1, Singapore's INTRACO, as a state trading enterprise, was modelled after the famed *sogo shosha* or GTCs in Japan. The nine GTCs in Japan are Itochu, Kanematsu, Marubeni, Mitsubishi, Mitsui, Nichimen, Nissho Iwai, Sumitomo and Tomen. In general, *sogo shosha* were regarded as quite distinct from the other wholesale businesses because of their huge size and their capacity to deal in 20,000 to 30,000 different products. These *sogo shosha* are also involved in production, intermediate and consumer goods. Their commercial dealings included both domestic and foreign transactions that were often efficiently integrated and would cover the entire distribution process (Uesugi and Yamashiro, 2006, p. 64). For example, in the case of textile transactions, the *sogo shosha* would run the gamut of cotton and wool purchases and imports to fibre, textile, clothing sales and exports. Often, these commercial transactions were supported by a variety of activities such as investment, financial and management assistance and information provision. Apart from neighbouring countries such as China and South Korea, such a model of operation is rarely seen outside Japan.

THE *SOGO SHOSHA* MODEL

Many countries had set out to emulate the *sogo shosha* because they thought the *shosha* were a crucial component of the Japanese economic model. To a certain extent, this is true because the *shosha* have a myriad system of networks with various companies in the domestic economy. However, while the *sogo shosha* played an important role with the domestic Japanese economy, international trade remains a core activity and this model has evolved beyond the scope of international trade intermediary (Larke and Davies, 2007). The intermediation role of *sogo shosha* takes the form of consulting, introduction and sourcing. The collective activities of the various groups within particular *sogo shosha* made them powerful in the Japanese economy. In the post-World War II era, *shoshas* were also able to extend credit lines to companies through their financial arms while simultaneously entrenching their linkages throughout the domestic economy. This meant that they were able to exercise influence through their banking arms even to the level of the small and medium enterprises (SMEs) in Japan.

How do we unravel the complexities of *sogo shosha* linkages? Agency theory explains the role of *sogo shosha* as brokers, by providing risk reduction in trading between partners, that tend to be geographically and culturally diverse (Larke and Davies, 2007). However, agency theory overlooks the fact that trading companies are frequently active as market-makers and value creators because of their ability to work in diverse markets. The capturing and transmitting of information was critical for the smooth management and distribution of the appropriate merchandise to customers (Torii and Nariu 2004, p. 4). However, the reduction of transaction costs as a result of trading over distances and through cultural and political barriers as provided by the *sogo shosha* was rather short-lived. Any competitive advantage gained will be eroded over time as both parties (suppliers and wholesalers) or third parties become capable of dealing directly with one another (Torii and Nariu, 2004, p. 4). In this context, the long-term survival and growth for trading companies would rely on their ability to create new and often diverse opportunities to maintain a widely dispersed network of businesses.

The *sogo shoshas* had thrived because they were able to fill the gaps in the highly dynamic distribution network. However, the consolidation of the fragmented distribution chain over time by other smaller traders would eventually close the "gaps" that *sogo shosha* were able to exploit. Moreover, with the increasing sophistication of the market, branded and specialised goods would require after-sales services that were not part of the traditional mode of *sogo shosha* operations. In the 1980s, *sogo shosha* were active as main licensors of overseas luxury brands, but this role has been surpassed over time when distribution rights from the suppliers in most cases were passed to sub-licensees. Thereafter, in addition to providing intermediary services to other retail companies, *sogo shoshas* aimed to exploit their own international supply chains and it could be argued that they were acting as marketing companies (Torii and Nariu, 2004, p. 4). As marketing companies, the *sogo shoshas* were planning for new merchandise to ensure profitable product choices for retailers. It became necessary for *sogo shoshas* to collect and analyse information on demand and supply and the relation between product quality and costs. Information concerning products provided by rival companies and on what terms were also useful (Torii and Nariu, 2004, p. 4).

Sogo shoshas, in their establishment of the "Develop and Import Scheme", realised that as importers, they needed to master a variety of functions in order to enable synergy in the smooth running of their large-scale development projects. This entailed the establishment of export facilities, machinery and materials for the specific project. With the expansion of their development projects, the requirements for a diverse range of commodities increased and it was the *sogo shosha*'s responsibility to locate and acquire these commodities and enterprises (Tanaka, 2009, p. 8).

Among *sogo shoshas*, despite their similarities, there are also vast differences and contrasting characteristics. For example, Mitsui & Co. is known for its international market knowledge and expertise gained through its extensive overseas offices (numbering 564) that spread across 79 countries. In contrast, Mitsubishi Corporation is famous for its diverse products — "from ramen to missiles". Superficially, these two companies may seem alike because Mitsubishi Corporation also has 500 overseas offices across 80 countries and Mitsui & Co. also offers a range of products. However, these figures do not reveal the respective companies' true expertise, nor is it a predominant paradigm that is shared by top management and filtered down to their employees (Cho, unpublished).

The key challenge for the *sogo shosha* was to remain relevant with increasing globalisation of markets and technological advancements in communication, transportation and banking. These changes in the global economy, coupled with ongoing internationalisation of manufactures and customers, have collectively led to the reallocation of many traditional distribution functions performed by international trade intermediaries (Ellis, 2001, p. 236). As a result, some scholars have labelled *sogo shosha* as irrelevant, having outlived their "usefulness". Defying their critics, such trading companies continue to prosper at the interstices of global markets.

What accounts for their continued relevance? The general, implicit assumption is that trading companies never grow to become anything other than highly diversified trading companies. However, the adaptive parameters may not be so narrowly defined. At the basic level, trading companies may diversify either forward or backward (Ellis, 2001, p. 240). Forward integration refers to the provision of additional services such as transportation, warehousing and insurance, whereas backward integration implies diversification into manufacturing so as to counter the threat of opportunism in the distribution channel. The tendency of trading companies to diversify away from trading has been evident from the earliest records of trading and arguably another evolutionary outcome when the company's principal activities begin to expand into areas other than trading. Such a change in strategic direction could be the result of diminishing opportunities for trade intermediation as the home economy matures.

The functions of *sogo shoshas* can therefore be classified into basic and extended. The basic functions were trading, financing and information gathering. Based on these three basic functions, *sogo shoshas* developed extended functions that are able to respond to the changing requirements of the global economy, and these included resource development, technology transfer and organisation.

In its simplest form, the function of trading activity is to stand between the suppliers and users of commodities or finished products as well as to facilitate the flow of commerce between the two entities at home and abroad. The *sogo shoshas* normally handled large-scale commodities such as raw materials, agricultural crops, oils and other products because the trading commission is very low, at about 2% of net sales or less.

In terms of financing, this could be classified into two types. The first is trade credits and the second is loans and investments. In Japan, banks often do not wish to take the risks of lending to financial companies because their financial standing may not be evident. Therefore, banks entrusted *sogo shoshas* with the ability to provide credit for smaller trading companies. This created opportunities for *sogo shoshas* to step in and offer trade credits, long- and short-terms loans, investments and guarantees for payment of credit.

The ability of *sogo shosha* to provide speedy and highly reliable information was important not only to develop new business opportunities, but also to build a good relationship with customers. *Sogo shoshas* were tasked by the state to develop their global information network in order to enable their companies to estimate and analyse first-hand information. In this regard, they will also have to co-operate with other agencies such as environmental offices, news organisations, think-tanks and other relevant institutions.

Sogo shoshas were evolving and responding to the changing requirements of the industrial society, and these were described as extended functions that included resource development for a resource-poor country such as Japan that depended on resources from foreign countries to fuel their exports. Technology transfer through their worldwide network was crucial for the continued development of the Japanese economy as well as establishing Japanese industries in developing economies. The state's role in the organisation of industries for the future was also crucial because *sogo shosha* needed to co-ordinate and streamline their various business entities. These could range from manufacturing, construction to engineering companies.

Should the need arise, the *sogo shoshas* also promoted joint projects overseas through a consortium of companies. Information was critical for the functioning of the *sogo shosha* and they often acted as a bridge between the wholesalers and retailers (Torii and Nariu, 2004, p. 9). The *sogo shoshas* were able to gather and analyse all the relevant information from their many retailing clients and source for the best-quality supplies at the lowest cost. They were also able to extend their role in logistics and supply chain through the storage and transportation of goods from wholesalers to retailers. In this context, the *sogo shoshas* were able to economise on costs for inventory and transportation.

ROLE OF THE STATE IN ECONOMIC DEVELOPMENT: BUREAUCRATS IN BUSINESS

Increasingly, globalisation and rapid development in technology have driven companies to search for sources of competitive advantage. One of the key prerequisites would be access that could provide the information for businesses to anticipate changes in the policy environment (Schuler *et al.*, 2002, p. 659). Access to officials with current and strategic information would also increase the company's ability to survive by decreasing uncertainty in the political domain. Analysts have pointed out that access is the principal goal of most interest groups and lobby groups have acknowledged that access is the key to persuading policy makers (Schuler *et al.*, 2002, p. 659).

How do companies, especially trading companies that are more vulnerable to external environment, gain access to markets? The role of external directors is one approach. Directors who are familiar with the legislative machinery could assist in the political dealings of a company by utilising their skills to predict government actions. Such skills could be acquired in two ways. First, it could come from prior participation in governmental activities with the knowledge of procedures, including ties with important decision makers. Second, it could be derived from experience in dealing with the government in an adversarial role in administrative or legal proceedings (Agrawal and Knoeber, 2001, p. 182).

External directors on corporate boards, if they perform effectively, would select, monitor, reward or punish managers. These activities assist in the alignment of managerial and shareholder interests. Moreover, many external directors are senior executives in other companies and possess considerable business acumen and decision-making skills. They would be able to do more with their expertise and knowledge of technologies and markets that their company managers may be less familiar with (Agrawal and Knoeber, 2001, p. 180). A significant number of these external directors would also have important non-business experience in government, academe, the arts, law and politics (Agrawal and Knoeber, 2001, p. 180). Agrawal and Knoeber argued that politics is an important determinant of a company's profitability because lawyers and those with political experience will aid the company with their knowledge of government procedures and insights in predicting government actions (Agrawal and Knoeber, 2001, p. 180). They could also enlist the government in the company's interest or to forestall government actions inimical to the company. However, influence could flow in the other direction too. Specialists on Japan routinely pointed out that the government used retired bureaucrats to influence business behaviour. The former bureaucrats also enabled the state to extend its visible and invisible influence throughout its jurisdiction (Miwa and Ramseyer, 2005, p. 315).

How important are the board of directors in influencing their companies' strategic planning and key decisions? The role of directors in providing advice and direction to companies based on their corporate experience and expertise is one way of evaluating their clout over the company's function. Another approach would be to assess their ability to act as intermediaries to counter problems or tensions that may arise between shareholders and the management. The emphasis on governance is another approach to examine the role of directors, especially bureaucrats or retired bureaucrats without any corporate experience (Raj and Yamada, 2009). Business, especially trading involves a certain measure of risk taking and being opportunistic. Generally, bureaucrats are risk averse and may not seize opportunities without clearance from their superiors.

JAPAN AND *AMAKUDARI*

In the Japanese corporate world, the system of *Amakudari* or literally, "descent from heaven", describes a practice to re-employ retired bureaucrats in the board of directors of private and public corporations (Raj and Yamada, 2009). Calder pointed out that retiring bureaucrats in Japan flowed from the central government ministries to various "landing spots", and the dynamics pushing them out of the bureaucracy into second careers are common in most cases (Calder, 1989, p. 382). The low purchasing power of post-war pay scales in bureaucracy and the upward pressure created by large numbers of lower-level officials seeking advancement were key drivers of the *Amakudari* system (Calder, 1989, p. 382). The convergence of these two primary reasons has caused Japanese bureaucrats from the 1960s to 1980s to retire between the ages of 45 and 55. Usually, none of these bureaucrats would continue in government service once members of their own cohort or junior cohort have attained the height of bureaucratic prominence, such as the administrative vice-ministership of their respective organisations (Calder, 1989, p. 382).

Calder also explained that the most critical function of most former bureaucrats in Japan would be in providing information to their adopted organisations concerning likely actions by their former employers and more general economic and political developments (Calder, 1989, p. 392). Japanese decision-making processes tend to be subtly hidden and personality-driven, with much strategic information relevant to corporate decision making only passing between social peers with long-standing personal linkages (Calder, 1989, p. 392). With the phase of lifetime employment, employees of private companies, especially those of small and medium enterprises (SMEs), often have limited contact outside of their own companies. Therefore, the intelligence-gathering capabilities of former bureaucrats proved very useful. These former bureaucrats employed by companies have a vast network of personal contacts, including memberships to research groups for politicians that could be mobilised for intelligence purposes. In the case of lower-level officials, they network extensively through the well-developed alumni associations of the various ministries.

In terms of intelligence gathering, in the 1950s and 1960s, former bureaucrats in the *Amakudari* system were mainly involved in domestic intelligence. This changed from the 1970s onwards when Japanese MNCs started expanding internationally and extended linkages with non-market-oriented socialist economies. Japanese companies increasingly became more conscious of the value of overseas contacts and information about potential foreign markets. In order to meet this demand from companies for specialised contacts and information, trade officials from Japan's Ministry of Trade and Industry and the Ministry of Foreign Affairs began flowing in large numbers to Japanese industrial and commercial enterprises. In the 1980s, the role of former bureaucrats in providing information on emerging government research programmes, prospective government research standards and future co-operative research between the private and public sectors became more important (Calder, 1989, p. 393). Retired government officials in Japan were also important in terms of assurance, as they were included to some extent to the normally exclusive network of bureaucratic consultation and compensation. In particular, this function was very important to small companies such as mutual savings banks and the telecommunications subcontractors of Nippon Telephone and Telegraph. The survival of these companies would be imperilled without the "cocoon" of government regulation that supported them. In the 1970s and 1980s, Japanese financial deregulation in areas such as savings rate liberalisation occurred at a glacial pace. This was partly because of the large number of staff — formerly from the Ministry of Finance and Bank of Japan — that were employed at the small and relatively non-competitive local banks, which tried to perform insurance functions on behalf of their adopted institutions (Calder, 1989, p. 393).

The former bureaucrats also performed roles as brokers. As Japan accelerated its economic development in a highly regulated government framework, population distribution and industrial structures were transformed. Regulatory patterns and economic realities had to be brokered to maintain growth. For instance, former bureaucrats from the Ministry of Finance helped secure licenses for new bank branches in the suburban prefectures around the capital city, Tokyo.

In the 2000s, the practice of *Amakudari* continues with retired bureaucrats playing a political role with their past experiences in government to provide knowledge of government procedures, identify the services wanted by government, leverage on contacts and personal relationships developed during their career span, and assist to facilitate interaction with government.

CHINA OFFICIALS AND *XIAHAI*

In a Cold War setting, China preferred to have business links with foreign state-owned enterprises like INTRACO because the Chinese government and its own state-owned enterprises were more comfortable trading business in that manner. However, this would change after China implemented its economic liberalisation, and after both countries established bilateral diplomatic relations in 1990.

Li explained the role of bureaucrats in business as the economics of *Xiahai*, literally, "descending into the open sea (of business)". Since 1992, *Xiahai* has been very popular among Chinese government officials (Li, 1998). These former bureaucrats obtained higher wages and personal freedom when they join the business world despite the economic uncertainty. There was high demand for these bureaucrats, because at the time, in the half-reformed liberalising economy, many private enterprises needed the bureaucrats' knowledge and skills to manage the remaining government regulations.

Xiahai seemed to have had a positive effect on China's economic reform process because it pushed for changes in the bureaucracy. The incumbent bureaucrats would establish a pro-business and pro-reform reputation, making it easier for them to find a good position in the corporate sector after leaving the government. One way to achieve this would be to promote growth and reform and to nurture personal ties with local entrepreneurs to help their businesses expand. In contrast, a bureaucrat that was anti-reformist will find it impossible to find a good position in the local business community after leaving government service. In addition, most Chinese bureaucrats upon leaving government service would join new businesses rather than state-owned enterprises. Therefore, for many of them, the bureaucratic regulations that they helped maintain in the bureaucracy might become obstacles to their future business interests (Li, 1998). They were also in a position to help circumvent and lobby for reductions to these bureaucratic regulations because they had the knowledge and skills to effectively lobby for reforms, as compared to outsiders to the system.

INTRACO IN SINGAPORE

Would bureaucrats make good managers? Fan *et al.* (2009) observed four broad patterns in their data regarding bureaucrats. First, CEOs who served as bureaucrats were more likely than other executives to enter new industries. Second, former civil servants who headed state-owned enterprises would choose a mixture of business activities that were largely at odds with the recommendations of scholars studying corporate strategy. Third, given the regularities, CEOs without government experience managing private companies make the most successful leaders. Fourth, private sector incentives can be more important than executives' career paths. In particular, civil servants in charge of private companies were statistically indistinguishable from executives without a bureaucratic past (Fan *et al.*, 2009).

Nonetheless, former civil servants have detailed knowledge of the government's inner workings and this would be valuable in a state-directed economy. Former bureaucrats would also have opportunities to personally know other officials and regulators, and this might influence their strategic decisions. In China, for example, former bureaucrats lead regulated businesses in the telecom and energy industries because of their familiarity with the regulatory processes and regulators. However, Fan *et al.* in their study found little evidence that shareholders benefited from the appointment of former bureaucrats to the position of CEO (Fan *et al.*, 2009). This group of senior executives did not outperform managers without government expertise. Moreover, there was consistent evidence that former bureaucrats underperformed when compared to their peers when they take charge of state-owned enterprises. In some cases, these former bureaucrats chose to compete in more challenging business sectors with lower profitability and growth rates. In the Chinese context, bureaucratic ties influence the strategic choices of companies and these choices have consequences for the short-run profitability and the sustainability of competitive advantage. Other studies focused on managerial style, organisational incentives and the company's competitive environment to understand variation in financial performance, while others concentrate on CEO personality and executive careers.

In the case of INTRACO, apart from having a board of directors, there was an executive committee of bureaucrats that provided advice on the company's directions and strategic planning. Raj and Yamada (2009) pointed out that the positive effects of having bureaucrats on the board of directors would be to leverage on their experience to help companies obtain and use government information more efficiently. The negative aspect would be that their personal relationships within government agencies could be used to win contracts or gather confidential information. Duckett argued that politicians and officials in the developing world often have lucrative interests based on their public positions and the networks that they established around them (Duckett, 2001, p. 24). INTRACO was established in Singapore to develop external linkages with the socialist and centrally planned economies like China.

Would INTRACO have fared better in terms of performance without the presence of civil servants in its ranks? The role of bureaucrats in business was a legacy from former Prime Minister Lee Kuan Yew. Academics like Anthony Shome argued that bureaucrats were more trusted than entrepreneurs to drive the economy (Shome, 2009, p. 322). Former PM Lee Kuan Yew believed that to succeed as an entrepreneur, one has to have extraordinary qualities because few were born entrepreneurs and not many will succeed. Therefore, state-guided entrepreneurship was the path taken to drive the Singapore economy. Senior bureaucrats were given leading roles in driving the economy because it was believed that they could be motivated to take on different tasks (Shome, 2009, p. 322).

Moreover, business is ideologically impartial, and trading happens everywhere and with anyone under mutually acceptable conditions (Shome, 2006, p. 26). In contrast, the state or government functions on an ideological basis especially during the Cold War. In this context, the Singapore government had no diplomatic relations with China until 1991. Therefore, INTRACO was a useful state-owned enterprise to establish and expand trading links with China and other socialist countries.

Picture 2.1. Board of Directors at INTRACO. (Photo courtesy of S. Chandra Das.)

STATE ENTREPRENEURIALISM

Arguably, the state-guided entrepreneurship in Singapore is a continuation of the commercial legacy left by the British. During the British colonial times, the government owned a range of companies in telecommunications, airlines, utilities, ports and shipyards. The commercial sector in Singapore post-independence was primarily occupied by shopkeepers, hawkers, moneychangers and general merchandise companies. The larger entrepreneurs were from the bureaucracy, but this experience did not nurture the development of private enterprises or transition to a free market. There is also a pervasive fear of failure in any form among Singaporeans. The stigma attached to failures and the propensity to "play it safe" was inimical to the creation of entrepreneurs (Shome, 2006). Hence, the government became heavily involved through the model of state entrepreneurship under the leadership of bureaucrats in sovereign wealth funds such as Temasek Holdings. Apart from the lack of entrepreneurship, the state also had to intervene because Singapore's location at

Picture 2.2. Board of Directors and Management at INTRACO. (Photo courtesy of S. Chandra Das.)

the confluence of the major-sea lanes made it an ideal meeting place for traders , which if properly capitalised would provide the impetus for economic development. Many well-known companies such as Britain's Borneo Company, Bousteads, Harrison Crossfields and Sandilands Butterys were established at the turn of the century (Shome, 2006).

The late Sim Kee Boon, who was Head of the Civil Service and Director of Temasek Holdings, and was instrumental in the establishment and management of INTRACO, had said, "Two decisions were made: invite multinational corporations to enter our market and get the government involved, to give confidence to the whole industrialisation effort. There was no conscious decision [as to] which industries the government would go into — we were even making pyjamas! The objective then was simply job creation. It was an eclectic and pragmatic policy" (Shome, 2006, p. 14). In this context, INTRACO supported this objective and became an exporting agent for locally produced goods and a bulk importer for raw materials required by local manufacturers.

CHAPTER 3

STATE-GUIDED CAPITALISM

"ENTREPRENEURIAL SHORTAGE" AND THE ROLE OF BUREAUCRATS IN THE ECONOMY

One of the main challenges the government faced during the post-Malaya separation period was that Singapore's entrepreneurial community consisted mainly of businessmen such as small-time traders and shopkeepers without experience in investing in factories or enterprises that required long gestation periods. Most of Singapore's government-linked companies (GLCs) were established in the late 1960s and 1970s during the initial phase of the country's economic development (Yahya, 2005, p. 4). This strategy was to compensate for the shortage of investible funds and expertise in the private sector to create new businesses and expand the economy (Ramirez and Tan, 2004, p. 512). While it could be argued from the point of view of traders that there were no shortages of entrepreneurial skills among them but the government's perspective was that it needed trusted individuals to implement Singapore's economic blueprint. The main source of trusted and capable individuals from the point of view of then Prime Minister Lee Kuan Yew was the Civil Service and in particular the elite Administrative Service.

In addition, Singapore's banks were reluctant to advance credit to these traders to start new businesses because its bankers did not have the experience or expertise to undertake risk assessments and manage these risks (Lee, 2002). More than a decade after its independence, in 1977, then Minister of State for Finance Goh Chok Tong said, "if we are going to make it on our own steam ... we should have our own expanding pool of local entrepreneurs. ... We must identify the reasons for the slow emergence of local industrialists" (Lim and Teoh, 1986, pp. 340–341). The following year, then Finance Minister Hon Sui Sen said, "We have yet to see any substantial development of local entrepreneurial ability in the manufacturing sector" (Lim and Teoh, 1986, p. 341).

A former director of INTRACO and a senior civil servant in the elite Administrative Service, Ngiam Tong Dow, said "Singapore's merchant-class were essentially traders. They were adept and agile in trading rubber, sugar and rice. They lacked the knowledge and technology in manufacturing, transportation or managing five star hotels. In critical areas, the State had no choice but to co-invest with private entrepreneurs, providing risk capital and access to technology" (Ngiam, 2005). The lack of entrepreneurs compelled the government to direct GLCs to establish key sectors of the economy and assume risks that the private sector was not able to withstand. Government ministers such as Dr Goh Keng Swee, Hon Sui Sen and Lim Kim San undertook the task of establishing such new enterprises.

Borne out of necessity, it was not considered unusual that government ministers acted as entrepreneurs, and they selected the most promising and energetic of civil servants to manage these companies (Lee, 2002). Ministers and civil servants were highly motivated to succeed in order to solve the issue of unemployment and create better living standards for citizens. Some of the key institutional agencies that had worked with INTRACO since the independence of Singapore would include the Trade and Development Board (TDB) that was established in 1983 and subsequently became International Enterprise (IE) Singapore, whose role was to promote trade and internationalisation of Singapore-based companies (Abeysinghe, 2007). Another key institution that had collaborated with INTRACO was the National Trades Union Congress, or NTUC. State-guided entrepreneurship, or "state entrepreneurialism", described the functions of government enterprises: when a state plays the role of entrepreneur, it is referred to as the entrepreneurial state and the bureaucrats are the entrepreneurial agents of the state (Shome, 2006, p. 4). However, observers have pointed out that as government-sponsored entities, GLCs have access to consular exchanges during their overseas business forays that can provide them with diplomatic contacts to facilitate their networking. GLCs also have access to government archives and data banks for quick dissemination of information (Shome, 2006, p. 25). For instance, the close relationship between INTRACO with TDB and then IE Singapore and the

Ministry of Foreign Affairs (MFA) had enabled INTRACO to establish networks with countries overseas especially within the Socialist Bloc.

Business involves high risk and funding of GLCs comes from taxpayers' money, which meant that losses incurred by GLCs were a depletion of the state treasury (Shome, 2006, p. 26). In this context, the board of directors and management committee at INTRACO had in principle to uphold the profit motive and the principle of sustainable business in the company's activities. However, in the case of INTRACO, which was in the trading business, the risks were greater because of the highly competitive nature of the business with narrow margins (often of not more than 5%) and the exposure to the uncertainty of global events.

For example, in 1985, in the midst of a recession and a global economic downturn, the board of directors and management committee at INTRACO had differences about the balance sheet and direction that INTRACO executives should take to expand the company. As will be elaborated in later chapters, this led to the exodus of senior executive from INTRACO and some would argue that this initiated the decline of the GLC.

CONTEXT AND PROCESS OF CHANGE MODEL

In the fledgling years of Singapore's economic development, INTRACO was seen as an iconic GLC. One approach to understand and assess the internationalisation role of INTRACO in Singapore's economic development is to use the Context of Change Model from management studies. Zutshi and Gibbons argued that the context of change is divided into inner and outer contexts (1998, p. 221). The outer context refers to the national economic and political environment in which changes are occurring, while the inner context refers to the strategy, structure and culture of the organisation. The process of change refers to the actions taken during change while the content of change refers to the specific changes studied. The Context of Change Model should be used in conjunction with emerging local and global events in order to understand the various factors that had influenced the development of INTRACO over the decades. Operating in a risky and ever evolving global trading system, INTRACO's actions and steps taken in response to changes and challenges ultimately shaped the company. This would then be linked to strategic planning and the resources

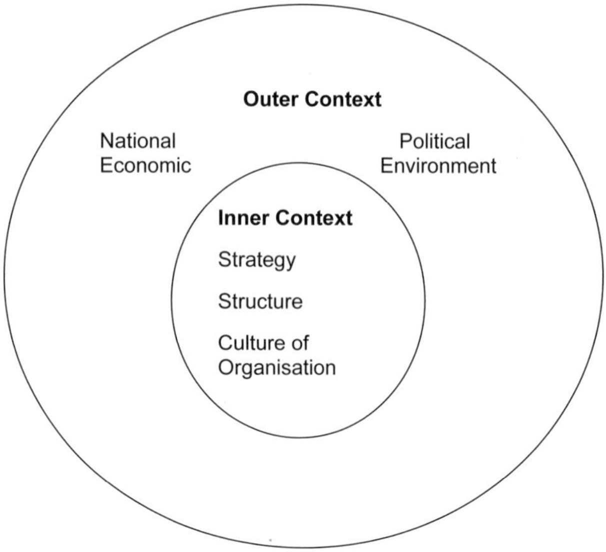

Figure 3.1. Context of Change Model.

and/or capabilities that the company would need to face these challenges. Figure 3.1 illustrates the Context of Change Model.

In the case of INTRACO, the company was influenced by both global events and policy changes in the domestic economy. In the 1960s, the main national objective was to curb unemployment through industrialisation and import substitution. During the Cold War, export-led growth was deemed to be critical and the attraction of foreign investment was paramount, and INTRACO was established as a conduit for Singapore to trade with China and the Soviet bloc. In the 1970s, the emphasis turned towards expanding the Singapore economy by exploring and exporting to overseas markets and procuring raw materials at bulk prices for local manufacturers (Zutshi and Gibbons, 1998, p. 221).

The 1980s signalled a shift in international trade with the ending of the Cold War, while the 1990s experienced greater trade liberalisation and economic integration of sovereign economies under the framework of the World Trade Organization (WTO). The political environment had a strong influence on INTRACO because of the development model of the Singapore economy, dubbed "Singapore Inc". Douglas Johnston explained "Singapore Inc" as the process of privatisation that sought to reduce the overloading of state institutions (Johnston, 2001, p. 5). This process of privatisation was also seen as an experiment to discover sectors where goods and services could be provided more efficiently by the corporate community with minimal intervention by the government apparatus. GLCs working under the parameters of the Singapore Inc model had to function as corporate entities and keep a close watch on their bottom line. In this regard, Singapore followed a developmental state model with a focus towards export-oriented industrialisation, and it required access to resources for manufacturing and markets overseas as export outlets. As the Singapore economy developed, the global economy changed with the rise of protectionism and efforts to liberalise the international trading regime.

Therefore, the Singapore Inc model as part of the country's development strategy had to establish links between the domestic economy and the international economic community, effectively this meant liberalising sectors of the local economy in keeping with its membership obligations under the General Agreement of Tariffs and Trade (GATT) and thereafter the WTO.

Shown later in Chapter 4, despite experiencing problems, without divesting its state-owned assets by the Public Sector Divestment Committee (PSDC), it would have been harder for Singapore to invest overseas in foreign-owned state enterprises or branded and high profile foreign companies (*The Straits Times*, 29 April 2000). Temasek Holdings and the PSDC divided the state-owned enterprises under its purview into core (strategic) and non-core (non-strategic) assets. The PSDC divested interests in non-strategic or non-core GLCs to meet Singapore's WTO commitments to liberalise its economy. This indirectly helped Singapore companies gain entry to overseas markets and invest in foreign state-owned or foreign branded companies. Moreover, the GLCs as envisioned by Dr Goh Keng Swee and under the model of Singapore Inc operate as private enterprises. Therefore, the state would not be able to have an interest in them indefinitely. The privatisation process was accelerated in the late 1980s.

SOVEREIGN WEALTH FUND TEMASEK HOLDINGS

A study by Stephen Appold (2002) on Singaporean business elites concluded that there was a clear pattern of core and periphery entities among GLCs: GLCs occupy the central positions in the network of companies while multinational companies (MNCs) and domestic companies occupy less important places in the network and linkages than their contribution to the economy would suggest (Appold, 2002). While in theory, it does not matter who owns the enterprise as long as it operated in a competitive market, in the long run, concerns would arise: all conditions for a competitive market are seldom achieved and even if they were achieved they would not be sustainable (Heracleous, 1999, p. 435).

How was INTRACO established? Prior to 1973, Development Bank of Singapore (DBS) Limited and INTRACO were the *de facto* holding companies for the government. In 1968, DBS was separated from the Economic Development Board (EDB) to become the national development financing institution and later a full-fledged commercial bank. In the same year, INTRACO was incorporated from existing operations within the EDB. In 1974, both INTRACO and DBS were incorporated into the portfolio of the government's main holding company, Temasek Holdings (Sikorski, 1989, p. 77). A number of Temasek Holdings managers were chosen from the civil service and military, and each were appraised and compensated according to their performance (Anwar and Sam, 2006, p. 51). Although used as an economic tool by the government, one of the criticisms levelled at GLCs was that because they were profit-driven, they had limited role in national welfare and lacked social responsibility. In terms of their future growth, it was narrowly pegged to shareholder interests and lacked altruistic objectives, and they may venture into areas that were not always congruent to national interests. Due to their historical role in facilitating sectoral economic development, some of the GLCs have also dominated particular sectors of the economy such as telecommunication and transportation. This has given rise to the perception that they are "crowding out" the rest of the private sector through their "overwhelming dominance" in the Singapore economy (Singapore Department of Statistics, 2001).

According to Ho Ching, the Executive Director of Temasek Holdings, the shares of these GLCs were held by Temasek Holdings from its inception in 1974 because the government wanted to prioritise and focus on policies that would promote businesses and economic development (Ho Ching, 2010). Although the chairmen, board members and part of the management team at these GLCs were civil servants, the government was not involved in the management of these companies but wanted them to be professionally managed and to adopt a commercially disciplined approach. Market forces and opportunities shaped the activities of these companies and not the agenda of policy makers or politicians. However, to be granted independence from state interference, at least in operational terms, the GLC must be trusted by the government. This is not unusual in the Asian context when trust and social networks help to facilitate a smooth and timely flow of information within the government (Anwar and Sam, 2006, p. 54).

Shome pointed out that GLCs, as the main beneficiaries of the state-guided entrepreneurship model, would prosper better than companies of similar stature in the corporate sector because they have access to more capital and resources and are able to write off losses more easily (2006). With their ability to buy in large volume, they could also purchase at record low prices and artificially inflate the market. The GLCs overseas would also have access to consular exchanges that provide them with the diplomatic linkages and access to institutional agencies' archives and other information. Linkages through the board of directors to governmental agencies are also beneficial to GLCs.

On the other hand, business remains high-risk and losses to GLCs will deplete state finances as they are funded by taxpayers. In the case of INTRACO, however, business is ideologically impartial and companies trade everywhere and with anyone under mutually acceptable conditions (Shome, 2006). In contrast, state relations are inherently ideological and are subjected to political differences that influence relations in other areas including trade. INTRACO's fate was also inextricably tied to Temasek Holdings one of the two Sovereign Wealth Funds (SWFs) of the Singapore government, the other being the Government of Singapore Investment Corporation, or GIC. Then Singapore Minister for Finance Dr Tony Tan made the first official announcement in March 1985 about the government's Privatisation and Divestment Policy. INTRACO's public listing in 1972 was in line with the government's approach towards privatisation. Arguably, within INTRACO, the public listing was meant to accumulate funds for its business expansion.

SINGAPORE'S TRANSNATIONAL COMPANIES

While some Singapore companies began operating overseas in the 1960s, it was only in the late 1970s that these companies gained their momentum to venture overseas as transnationals (Lim and Teoh, 1986, p. 336). INTRACO was part of this group of companies that had ventured into overseas investments to secure material and to promote exports to third countries. INTRACO in Malaysia was involved in marble extraction with other Malaysian partners, while in Indonesia, it sourced timber for trading (Lim and Teoh, 1986, p. 332). The company's other foreign operations included oil palm cultivation and milling in China to obtain edible oil for trading. In South Asia, INTRACO was involved in the manufacturing of garments in Bangladesh for export to other countries. While it could be argued that the products of Singapore transnational corporations are equivalent in quality to those in developed economies, the former was handicapped in terms of marketing. Therefore, Singapore transnational corporations like INTRACO had manufactured products for transnational corporations in developed economies. For example, INTRACO had produced garments for Sears-Roebuck and Macy's (Lim and Teoh, 1986, p. 364).

PRIVATISATION PROGRAMMES

Some important economic conditions that facilitate successful privatisation would be an open trade regime, a stable and predictable environment for investment and a well-developed institutional and regulatory capacity. Market conditions also influence successful privatisation. Privatised enterprises that produced tradables or operated in competitive or potentially competitive markets could lead to improved efficiency, provided the divesture was conducted transparently. The privatisation of state-owned enterprises that operated as monopolies are more complex and the regulatory capabilities of the country becomes a crucial factor. Similarly, the privatisation of utilities and natural monopolies is most difficult in the least developed countries, or LDCs, in which institutional and regulatory capacities are weakest.

The PSDC that was established by Temasek Holdings had published its recommendations in 1987 on the privatisation of GLCs and statutory boards (Saunders and Lim, 1990, p. 292). The privatisation process in Singapore was aimed at broadening and deepening the Singapore stock market through the listing of the shares of these companies and statutory boards. Critics have argued that privatisation is not an automatic solution to improving the quality of goods and services available to businesses or the performance of state-owned enterprises. Contrary to expectations, the sale of state-owned enterprises should not be solely guided by how much revenue they will generate. It will be shown in later chapters, that the divestment of INTRACO was not based on the share price per unit but on the strategic purpose of the company. In the divestment process, it is important to develop clear criteria in selecting appropriate assets (Forfás, 2010). These were vital in ensuring that infrastructure users' interests are protected by not selling natural monopolies such as gas pipelines, key airports, electricity transmission lines and others or assets, to dominant competitors (Forfás, 2010).

It is important to ensure that investments in advanced infrastructure and regional development are promoted and regulatory capabilities are sufficiently advanced to achieve public policy objectives in the absence of ownership rights. When the conditions are appropriate to privatise a state-owned enterprise (SOE), there is a strong case for opportunistically divesting state assets when conditions in financial markets are favourable. If the state is to sell any of its state-owned enterprises, it is important that direct and indirect costs are minimised to ensure taxpayers benefited fully from any decision to privatise (Forfás, 2010).

Although the state has assumed a proactive entrepreneurial role by establishing the GLCs, they were to operate entirely as profit-driven commercial entities. Unlike most other state-owned enterprises in newly independent former colonial states at the time, that were either nationalised or established with political objectives, Singapore's GLCs were expected to provide commercial returns in line with the risks taken.

As a developing economy in the late 1960s, Singapore had encountered various problems in overseas markets and created GLCs such as INTRACO to facilitate its developmental objectives abroad. In particular, INTRACO was meant to spearhead Singapore's export promotion and trading on a bulk basis with socialist countries. The company was incorporated on 5 November 1968 with an authorised capital of S$50 million and was jointly owned by the

Picture 3.1. Singapore's Minister of Finance Hon Sui Sen, Sim Kee Boon (Chairman), Goh Tjoei Kok (Deputy Chairman) and S. Chandra Das (Managing Director). (Photo courtesy of S. Chandra Das.)

Singapore government, DBS and other private entities. Subsequently, INTRACO became Singapore's leading state trading enterprise[1] and expanded into a diversified group with manufacturing and trading subsidiaries ("Diversification from INTRACO" 1979). Unlike the 1960s and 1970s,

---

[1] Article XVII of the General Agreement on Tariffs and Trade (GATT) refers to three types of trading enterprises: (i) enterprises owned by the state, (ii) enterprises granted special privileges by the state in the form of a monopoly or subsidy equivalent and (iii) enterprises granted exclusive privileges by the state in the form of production, consumption or trade of certain goods. For the WTO, the definition of state trading enterprises is as follows: "governmental and non-governmental enterprises, including marketing boards, which have been granted exclusive or special rights or privileges including statutory or constitutional powers, in the exercise of which they influence through purchases or sales the level or direction of imports or exports". Three fundamental elements are identified in this working definition: (i) a governmental or non-governmental entity, including marketing boards; (ii) the granting to the enterprise of special rights or privileges and (iii) a resulting influence through the enterprise's purchases or sales, on the level or direction of imports or exports.

Picture 3.2. INTRACO Function — Hon Sui Sen (Minister of Finance), S. Chandra Das (Managing Director) and Lam Peck Heng (Assistant General Manager). (Photo courtesy of S. Chandra Das.)

newer GLCs in the 1980s to 1990s were formed in a different manner, mainly through the process of corporatisation of former government departments and statutory boards (Singapore Department of Statistics, 2001).

GLCs were diversified in nature and found in several industries in the domestic market. At a time when private enterprises in certain industries were not forthcoming, GLCs served as a critical vehicle of state entrepreneurship. For GLCs that experienced difficulties penetrating overseas markets, the pressure to make profits resulted in their aggressive expansion in the domestic market, which in turn led to concerns of their crowding out local companies in the domestic economy and magnifying the resource constraints and limitations of a city-state economy (Sabhlok, 2001, p. 21). There were also concerns among private enterprises and MNCs that GLCs would receive privileged treatment.

Picture 3.3. INTRACO's 15th Anniversary — Hon Sui Sen (Minister of Finance), Goh Tjoei Kok (Chairman) and Ngiam Tong Dow (Deputy Chairman). (Photo courtesy of S. Chandra Das.)

However, the government was adamant that GLCs received no special treatment (Sikorski, 1989, p. 74). This was emphasised by Dr Goh Keng Swee who said that GLCs should be run like private businesses and unsuccessful enterprises should be allowed to fail. In 1979, then Minister of Trade and Industry Goh Chok Tong went a step further when he said that the state should divest itself of these GLCs once they have succeeded (Sikorski, 1989, p. 76). As shown in later chapters, this rationale preceded the Privatisation and Divestment Policy in 1985.

Between 1985 and 1986, the Economic Committee set up by the Ministry of Trade and Industry led by Singapore's current prime minister, Lee Hsien Loong, provided a detailed plan to re-establish Singapore's level of competitiveness in response to the economic recession in 1985, experienced for the first time since independence. It suggested, among other things, that Singapore's economy should be led by the private sector, with suggestions to divest and privatise GLCs and statutory boards.

REORIENTING THE ROLE OF GLCs

The use of GLCs to develop and expand the Singapore economy has often come under intense scrutiny by the corporate sector and especially small and medium enterprises (SMEs). In his 2002 Budget Speech, then Minister of Finance Lee Hsien Loong, apart from reiterating that GLCs were not given special privileges or favours or burdened with "national service" responsibilities (uneconomic activities), elaborated on the government's plans for GLCs. The then Minister of Finance Lee explained that, "the Government in Singapore for historical reasons also participates in business through its interests in the Government-Linked Companies (GLCs), many of which have played critical roles in Singapore's economic development". In some instances with regards to the GLCs, he commented that, "The GLCs attract considerable attention, as well as a fair share of controversy. One possible reason for this is that the raison d'etre of the GLCs has not been explicitly spelt out and accepted". Minister Lee reiterated that, "the GLCs operate as commercial entities. The Government does not interfere with the operations of the GLCs. The companies are supervised by their respective boards of directors, who are accountable to their shareholders, including the Government. Nonetheless, in its Charter of 2002, Temasek Holdings did specify that it "will exercise shareholder rights to influence the strategic directions of its companies" (Temasek Charter, 2002). The Government will not favour GLCs with special privileges or hidden subsidies" (Ministry of Finance, 2002).

How would the divestment process be implemented? Since its founding, Temasek has steadily divested its stake in companies which are no longer strategic to Singapore or relevant to Temasek's mission. In addition, Temasek has also publicly listed major companies that have evolved from statutory boards such as Keppel Corporation and Singapore Telecommunications. Temasek companies have also divested their non-core assets and listed some of their major shareholdings over the years (Temasek Charter, 2002).

The government would assume a pragmatic approach and pay close attention to the prevailing industry and market conditions. For example, in the area of electricity generation, once the electricity market was operationally ready, the government would divest its electricity-generating

Table 3.1. Group and Company Profits for INTRACO from 2000 to 2004.

		Group			Company		
	Year	**First half**	**Second half**	**Total**	**First half**	**Second half**	**Total**
Turnover (S$'000)	2000	271,466	262,009	533,475	42,075	22,448	64,523
	2001	293,543	232,803	526,346	22,458	32,255	54,713
	2002	175,248	165,586	340,834	34,206	25,878	60,084
	2003	—	—	285,340	—	—	17,792
	2004	—	—	394,567	—	—	19,796
Profit/loss before tax (S$'000)	2000	17,280	(17,906)	(626)	14784	(17624)	(2,840)
	2001	(27,801)	(25,186)	(52,987)	(16,830)	(26,610)	(43,440)
	2002	3,738	(20,077)	(16,339)	2,537	(13146)	(10,609)
	2003	—	—	(7,549)	—	—	(4,595)
	2004	—	—	1,481	—	—	306
Profit/loss after tax (S$'000)	2000	15,875	(14,224)	1,651	14,784	(13,103)	1,681
	2001	(28,153)	(25,584)	(53,737)	(16,830)	(26,610)	(43,440)
	2002	3,648	(20,691)	(17,043)	2,537	(13,485)	(10,948)
	2003	—	—	(7,294)	—	—	(4,326)
	2004	—	—	1,007	—	—	306

companies such as Power Seraya, Power Senoko and Tuas Power (Ministry of Finance, 2002).

In the case of INTRACO, in the period of divestment by the state, investors in general became wary and cautious after INTRACO incurred considerable losses from 2001 to 2003 (Table 3.1). Could this have led to its total divestment in 2003? INTRACO was owned by a few large shareholders that included other GLCs, such as DBS and Natsteel. I would argue that the momentum for INTRACO's divestment could not be prevented because DBS was actively divesting its non-core businesses during that period. Strangely, DBS was also acting as the financial advisor for INTRACO Ltd. The other major shareholder of INTRACO was Natsteel that owned about 20% of INTRACO Ltd.

What was interesting to see was that before INTRACO was divested completely in 2003, the CEO of INTRACO Ltd, Teng Theng Dar, had earlier bought the company's share at above $0.97 but had reportedly liquidated the shares at below its cost of $0.67. Analysts speculated that he did not want to be seen to be benefitting from the high cash payout. Several criticism were hurled at INTRACO for its poor company results. Apart from the divestment by large shareholders, INTRACO was also accused of incurring losses by not focusing on its core business. For instance, the company had tried to invest in new businesses such as IT and media. Unfortunately, INTRACO's foray into the IT industry through Teledata Ltd however turned out to be a poor decision that resulted in substantial losses.

Another important point to note was the "criss cross" ownership pattern among GLCs. In this context, the majority shareholder in any specific GLC were often other GLCs and/or Temasek Holdings. For example, on 30 June 2003, when INTRACO was to be completely divested by the government, Natsteel (a GLC) had owned 21.42% equity interest in INTRACO, which was valued at S$8.5 million. On 21 November 2003, Natsteel sold its 6,816,990 ordinary shares of INTRACO at S$0.50 for a share consideration of S$0.52 per share. On the same day, Natsteel also accepted an offer from PSC Corporation Ltd to sell to PSC 14,309,260 of INTRACO shares for approximately S$8.87 million. The sale was arrived at mutual buyer-willing seller basis (Natsteel Limited, 2003). The divestment was in line with Natsteel's objective to focus on its core businesses and was not expected to have any material impact on the net tangible assets or earnings of the Natsteel Group. After INTRACO was divested by Natsteel and DBS, it sold 29.9% of its subsidiary Teledata Limited to Anchorage Asset Limited at S$6,190,237. In the government's Budget Speech of 2004, it was reported that its final ownership of INTRACO was 0% (Ministry of Finance, 2002). Interestingly after the GLCs' divestment of its shares, INTRACO's shareholding interest of Teledata, the company in which INTRACO incurred substantial losses, was reduced from approximately 50.65% to 20.75% and Teledata ceased to be a subsidiary of the company (INTRACO Limited, 2004).

Chapter 4 covers the first decades of INTRACO's development and is the first of three that examines in a chronological order the development and demise of INTRACO as a GLC. It will examine and highlight key factors that shaped and influenced INTRACO's development. The 1960s to 1980s, during the height of the Cold War, created several business opportunities for INTRACO. It also became a training ground for entrepreneurs.

This critical period also reflected the close linkages between the government-linked corporations and the government, with the expansion of state entrepreneurship. The following chapters also aim to examine the extent to which INTRACO tried to emulate the *sogo shosha* model. They seek to answer this key question: in changing global economic conditions, what was the impact of state-guided entrepreneurship on INTRACO's ability to evolve and thrive?

CHAPTER 4

"NATIONAL SERVICE" — 1960s TO 1980s

EVOLVING ROLE OF STATE-OWNED ENTERPRISES

The post-independence era brought huge challenges to the government. While the withdrawal of the British forces provided the government with additional assets in terms of military bases, it also resulted in thousands of people being unemployed. Such assets that could have been privatised were retained in the public sector for future use. As Singapore started on its economic path of export-oriented industrialisation and began to integrate with the global economy, efforts were made to expand and modernise infrastructure to attract foreign investments. To enable these government-linked corporations to make profit-oriented and timely decisions, administrative structures were kept simple with parent companies and their subsidiaries co-ordinated at the apex between chairmen and the board of directors. These chairmen and some of the board members were often senior civil servants drawn from a very small pool of trusted individuals and were in the network to integrate policy decisions with national priorities (Zutshi and Gibbons, 1998, p. 299).

The founding chairman of INTRACO, Sim Kee Boon, developed INTRACO's role as the state trading company and had the company listed in 1972. INTRACO became a place for senior bureaucrats to accumulate trading experience and gain insights into international trade practices. For example, INTRACO spearheaded Singapore's countertrade with the former Eastern European countries, the USSR, Africa and the Middle East. INTRACO's role facilitated Singapore's trade during the

Cold War in a divided global economy between the Western and Soviet Blocs. In examining the intentions and aspirations of the founding leaders of INTRACO, some key questions include: What were their strategic objectives? How did the state support INTRACO's foray overseas as a pathfinder, if at all?

In the words of Dr Goh Keng Swee, then Deputy Prime Minister and Finance Minister, in order to "blaze its own trail" overseas, it was necessary for INTRACO to have an appropriate strategy (Goh Keng Swee, Singapore Parliamentary Debates, 1968).

In a highly dynamic and complex external environment, a company's survival and expansion is dependent upon its ability to understand the environment and react in a timely manner in undertaking organisational adjustments (Luo and Tan, 1998, p. 25). The environmental dimensions would affect the fundamental management philosophies and principles to trigger a genuine review of corporate business operations. According to the neo-contingency model, good linkages between strategic orientation and environmental conditions in a turbulent context could enable the company to maximise the economic rents from the interaction between the "societal effect" and the "organisational effect" (Luo and Tan, 1998, p. 25).

In the early 1970s, earlier priority areas such as defence and shipyards had given way to diversification across a broad range of sectors in the economy. Government economic activities were being corporatised or sub-contracted, and this gave opportunities for government-linked corporations to expand their domains (Zutshi and Gibbons, 1998, p. 229). Due to more competition and decreasing demand, traditional industries such as the ship repair business had limited scope for expansion. The armament supply business was also unpredictable and had considerable impact on foreign policy. Therefore, the economy had to diversify from traditional entrépot trade to manufacturing, construction and other activities like tourism and financial services. One of the main benefits was that a decade of high growth in the 1970s led to a drop in unemployment rates and an increase in per capita income. The growth of some state-owned enterprises or government-linked corporations started to decrease in the 1980s because of moves by the government and this became more transparent later on when the privatisation policy was announced in

March 1985 (Sikorski, 1989, p. 80). The process of privatisation is usually influenced by several factors, but the key reason would be the generally disappointing performance of state-owned enterprises in terms of efficiency and profitability. Developing countries such as Singapore relied more heavily on the state-owned enterprises than developed economies (Heracleous, 1999, p. 433).

PUBLIC LISTING

In December 1972, INTRACO was publicly listed and its initial public offering was priced five times above its share offer price ("Severe setback for INTRACO", 1973). The shares were underwritten by Development Bank of Singapore (DBS)–Daiwa Securities International and backed by assets of S$1.31 each. Two million shares were on offer and 300,000 were reserved for the directors of INTRACO and its executives ("INTRACO offers 2 m shares for sale", 1972). INTRACO's directors announced that apart from trading activities, which were expected to grow as the scale of the company's operation expanded domestically and abroad, a satisfactory source of income from trade investments was also expected (INTRACO, 1973, pp. 4–6). In 1971, INTRACO's profits of S$3.1 million were exceptional due to the group's success in international tenders ("INTRACO offers 2 m shares for sale", 1972).

INTRACO shares were eagerly purchased, but by May 1973, the price had dropped to S$3.32 due to a sluggish market ("Severe setback for INTRACO", 1973). While it was expected that INTRACO's profits would suffer a setback in 1972, the 60% fall had caught analysts by surprise. Why the concern for a trading company during a volatile global economic environment? The accepted practice for newcomers to public listing would be to provide more modest projections than needed. However, before INTRACO reported a first half-year pre-tax profit of S$697,000 in 1972, even the most pessimistic observers had believed they would report at least double the figure of S$1.39 million as profits by the end of the year. The lower than expected pre-tax profits led some observers to believe that the issuing house was highly audacious in its strategic timing that caught positive market sentiments about INTRACO at the right time ("Severe setback for INTRACO", 1973).

In 1975, Sim Kee Boon, the founding chairman and managing director of INTRACO, was recalled to the Ministry of Finance. Goh Tjoei Kok, who was deputy chairman since INTRACO's inception, took over the helm as chairman. Goh Tjoei Kok came to Singapore from Djambi, Sumatra in the 1950s. His company Tat Lee was a major rubber and palm oil trader with plantations both in Indonesia and Malaysia. He and his business partners had established Singapore's first steel re-rolling mill called the National Iron and Steel Mills (NISM). NISM produced steel bars from ship scrap for Singapore's HDB housing programme. Other senior management reshuffle included Loo Siew Poh, who was the deputy managing director, became managing director. G. E. Bogaars continued in his position as Chairman of the Executive Committee and at the same time assumed the position of the Deputy Chairman of the Board (Directorate of INTRACO Ltd, 1974). Why is the movement of senior executives significant? Some of the former INTRACO executives interviewed for this research had expressed the belief that had Sim Kee Boon remained at INTRACO, the chances of INTRACO succeeding would have been greater, and that it could have become another Keppel Corporation under the guidance of Sim.

On another note, senior management and leadership also plays a critical role in the development of any organisation and INTRACO is no exception. Ngiam Tong Dow recalled that Goh Tjoei Kok had told him that INTRACO would never succeed because "the company's management was earning expatriate salary and doing small Chinese business" (Ngiam, 2005). Goh Tjoei Kok was implying that while INTRACO's executives were expecting to be paid world class salaries, they were not delivering world class performances.

PROFITS DRIVEN BY EXTERNAL EVENTS

The influence of global economic conditions on INTRACO is often overlooked when the company performed well. Between 1974 and 1975, global events such as oil shocks and global recession influenced INTRACO's profits strongly. In 1976, INTRACO's group pre-tax profit slumped to S$1.9 million, a drop of 56%, but at the parent company level, INTRACO's profit was S$2.33 million ("A bad year for INTRACO", 1975). This indicated that INTRACO's subsidiaries were not meeting expectations. However, INTRACO's reserves and assets were valued at S$30.2 million and 50% were tied to cash. Therefore, INTRACO was seen as an unfocused company with massive internal funds for expansion; and since 1972, the company saw a sizeable return of profits into its reserves ("A bad year for INTRACO", 1975). From 1972 to 1974, INTRACO's ration of current assets against current liabilities was at the ideal figure of two. However, INTRACO's shares saw very little movement on the stock market.

In relation to its main subsidiaries, INTRACO-owned Alpha Industries and Metraco had incurred losses. Alpha's main business was to supply ready-mix concrete to the building sector, and it had incurred a loss of S$318,000. Metraco manufactured rolled galvanised and steel roofing sheets and suffered losses of S$66,046. Two other subsidiaries, Seasonal Garments and Metrawood, which produced jeans clothing and knockdown furniture components, were profitable ("A bad year for INTRACO", 1975).

Despite the sluggish international economy, in 1978, INTRACO group sales continued to improve to a record S$98.17 million — up from S$94.04 million in 1977 — while pre-tax profits rose 2% to S$2.91 million. INTRACO chairman Goh Tjoei Kok[1] explained that the proliferation of protectionist policies in developed countries, together with the decrease in consumer spending and the lack of new investments, had caused the tapering off in growth rates in most economies (Sabnani, 1978). To maintain profit margins in a challenging environment, Goh explained that steps were taken to intensify marketing efforts overseas and priority was given to strengthening of contacts with overseas representatives (Sabnani, 1978). Despite sluggish economic conditions and trade barriers established by most developed countries, the trading sector performed well. INTRACO had established a special trading division that was divided between the chemical and general merchandise departments, and the

---

[1] Goh Tjoei Kok, a businessman, was originally from northern Sumatra, Indonesia. He had earlier answered Dr Goh Keng Swee's call to undertake the risk with some others to co-invest in the establishment of the National Iron and Steel Mill. See Tan (2007). *Goh Keng Swee: A Portrait.* Editions Didier Millet, p. 94.

former's tasks were centered on petroleum products ("INTRACO makes headway", 1979).

"NATIONAL SERVICE" — RICE STOCKPILE SCHEME

Although, then Minister of Finance Lee Hsien Loong had mentioned in his Budget Speech in 2002 that the government did not burden the government-linked companies (GLCs) with "national service" or uneconomic activities, INTRACO did undertake "national service" on the rare occasion. As Singapore's state trading enterprise, INTRACO was also called upon several times by the government to undertake measures that contributed to economic, political and social stability. Such actions were called "national service" among INTRACO executives. An example was the creation of a rice stockpile. Prior to 1974, the local rice trade was in the hands of the private traders. The government had kept a small amount of rice preserved by lime but this affected its taste and discoloured the rice. Thereafter, the rice became inedible and the government had to dispose of these rice stocks. The catalyst for the creation of a rice stockpile was the shortage of rice supply in Singapore in 1974. This shortage of supplies in rice forced the government to purchase a substantial quantity of rice at inflated prices established by rice traders. The inflated prices of rice in Singapore was due to the sharp increase in the prices of Thai rice in 1973 and 1974 caused by bad rice harvests in Thailand and the failure by the Thai Board of Trade to honour their contracts to rice merchants overseas. The adverse impact of the shortage was further accentuated when local importers exploited the situation through a cartel and sharply increased the price of rice further. As rice was the staple diet for most Singaporeans and Thailand was the main source of rice, the government became very concerned about the shortages and its potential to trigger social unrest in Singapore.

How could the government prevent and/or mitigate adverse conditions for rice supply shortages? In 1974, the government established a rice contingency fund and appointed INTRACO Ltd as the government's agent, through the Ministry of Trade and Industry, to import rice and maintain stable prices and strategic supplies for emergencies. Since then, the government had operated a rice stockpile scheme and a rice credit line from another GLC, DBS Limited, was made available. Its main objective was to ensure sufficient supplies of rice in the event of disrupted supply. At that point in time, about S$45 million worth of credit was obtained and the interest payments for that year totaled more than S$5 million. However, the sales of rice did provide profit for the stockpile and a contingency fund had been built, from S$7.475 million at the end of 1974 to S$36.638 million by the end of 1979. Part of the contingency fund was placed in a fixed deposit and the government stockpile was also able to earn interests.

Under the initial scheme in 1974, the number of private rice suppliers was limited to 16 importers. These rice importers were required to deposit part of their supplies with the stockpile for government-to-government purchased standard grade rice from Thailand on guaranteed credit terms and prices stipulated by the government. In addition, the government sold rice directly to the labour union's supermarkets (i.e., SILO and Welcome supermarkets) and the consumer clubs, which reduced the influence that the rice cartel has on consumers. According to one of INTRACO's director at the time, Baey Lian Peck, the consumer clubs were created by various Members of Parliament (MPs) at the time for essential items such as rice and sugar in order to show that they cared for the aged and the poor (Ooi, 2011, pp. 59–60).

INTRACO was responsible for the stockpiling of rice and maintained an initial stockpile of four and a half months' supply from its original aim of six months due to difficulties in stock rotation.

In late 1979, Thailand experienced drought in its rice growing regions. This resulted in large price increase of major grades of rice exported from Thailand. The huge increase in price was sustained in 1980 when the Thai government imposed measures to slow down its rice exports to boost prices in the latter half of the year. The Singapore government purchased primarily Thai 100% wholegrain grade B rice on a government-to-government basis. At the time, Singapore's dependency on Thai rice was well known and 90% of its rice was imported from Thailand. Why the dependency on Thai rice? Singapore consumers at the time found rice from other source countries either unpalatable or too expensive. This placed Singapore in a vulnerable position because the price of Thai rice had steadily risen between 1977 and 1981, as shown in a study in Table 4.1.

Table 4.1. Historical Prices for Thai 100% Wholegrain Grade B Rice, 1977–1981.

Period	Average price for period (US$ pmt)	Change in average price (US$ pmt)	Price at which purchases were made in period (US$ pmt)	Volume purchased (mt)	Change in volume purchased (mt)	Savings from purchase (US$ pmt) (2)–(4)	% Savings pmt (2)–(4) / (2)
1977							
Q1	272.27	—	250.00	7,500	—	22.27	8.2
Q2	272.65	0.38	257.00	5,000	−2,500	15.65	5.8
Q3	287.97	15.32	—	—	−5,000	—	—
Q4	307.65	19.98	272.5	5,000	5,000	35.45	11.5
1978							
Q1	382.00	74.05	332.50	22,000	17,000	49.50	13.0
Q2	422.17	40.17	—	—	−22,000	—	—
Q3	388.58	−33.59	—	—	0	—	—
Q4	337.92	−5.1	—	—	0	—	—
1979							
Q1	319.00	−18.92	300.00	20,000	20,000	19.00	6.0
Q2	333.70	14.7	310.00	10,000	−10,000	23.70	7.1
Q3	359.17	25.47	—	—	−10,000	—	—
Q4	383.30	24.13	353.00	15,000	15,000	30.30	7.9
1980							
Q1	417.00	33.7	400.00	15,000	0	17.00	4.1
Q2	442.03	25.03	413.00	15,000	0	29.03	6.6
Q3	450.00	7.97	—	—	−15,000	—	—
Q4	466.25	16.75	431.10	30,000	30,000	35.15	7.5
1981							
Q1	490.28	24.03	—	—	−30,000	—	—
Q2	532.67	42.39	515.00	15,000	15,000	17.67	3.3
Weighted average	388.14	—	363.00	—	—	25.14	6.5

The price of Thai 100% wholegrain grade B rice had risen from US$250 per metric tonne in 1977 to US$515 per metric tonne in 1981. The change in average price was steepest between the last quarter of 1977 to the first quarter of 1978 at US$74.05 per metric tonne.

The purchasing decision of INTRACO in administering the rice stockpile scheme and the Department of Trade were dependent on the price of rice set by the Thai Board of Trade authorities. The shorter periods of decreased prices were due to bumper harvests and a desire on the part of the Thai government to keep prices down to increase market share in certain buyer countries. However, decision makers in buying countries like Singapore operated in an uncertain environment with strategies formulated on rice purchases that were based on information that sometimes may not lead to expected results. For example, in June 1977, Singapore buyers guessed that prices would rise and stockpiled 5,000 tonnes of Thai 100% grade B rice at US$257, and prices indeed rose. On the other hand, the forecast of a bumper crop in the fourth quarter of 1977 had prudently advised local traders from securing further purchases in that year. However, when the bumper crop occurred, prices did not fall but instead rose and in 1978, the Department of Trade and INTRACO was forced to buy Thai 100% grade B rice because the stocks were being depleted below acceptable strategic levels.

The vagaries of purchasing decisions meant that Singapore buyers were constrained by the minimum stockpile level and imperfect information. The information sources at that point in time were as good as can be, short of perhaps information from the Thai Board of Trade itself. The Singapore government decided that the irrationality of purchases as indicated by the correlation coefficients should be reduced. This concern led the government to task the Department of Trade and INTRACO to monitor the rice demand and supply situation in Thailand, other ASEAN countries as well as Hong Kong, at the time the other major buyer of Thai fragrant rice. The Department of Trade and INTRACO were also tasked to monitor new sources of rice and to stay in close contact with Singapore's Bangkok rice agent, local importers and Thai exporters for market intelligence on prices quoted and expected trends. Singapore was compelled into entering into rice negotiations two to four times a year when stocks fell below the minimum targeted stock levels of four months' worth of rice. The contracts of purchases for rice delivery seldom stretched beyond a six-month period because of uncertainty on the Thai side.

Since it was not possible to conduct frequent rice negotiations in Bangkok, price negotiations conducted with Thai exporters at the time were undertaken from Singapore via telex through INTRACO's agent — Chareon Watana. Besides advising INTRACO on the domestic prices of jasmine rice in Bangkok and competitiveness of Freight-on-Board prices of various rice brands, Chareon Watana also checked the quality of rice for export. In January 1983, the government, through INTRACO, created a more formal channel to import rice from Thailand. A joint venture Siam-Sintraco Pte Ltd was incepted as a trading company in Thailand; and in May 1983, this was registered as a licensed rice company with the Department of Foreign Trade. Diversification of Singapore's sources for its rice supply became an imperative and trade missions were dispatched to purchase rice from non-traditional sources such as Pakistan and Taiwan.

Initially, INTRACO imported white rice but it subsequently imported jasmine rice, starting from 1983, due to lower volume of imports by private licensed traders. Between 1974 and 1986, INTRACO maintained separate accounts for the government and the company's commercial trading activities. INTRACO made a surplus of over S$100 million from the rice operations for the government's financial reserves. In 1985, after the Economic Committee's review during the recession, the government decided to restructure the rice stockpile scheme. In 1986, under the new scheme, the government, through INTRACO, ceased the import and stockpile of rice and the rice import market was opened to all companies. In return, all the rice importers who were licensed had to store twice their monthly import volume in newly-built government warehouses.

With the privatisation of INTRACO, Container, Warehousing and Transportation Private Limited (CWT) was appointed to manage the government's rice warehouses from 1986 to 1987 under the revised rice stockpile scheme. In 1987, the government decided to corporatise the rice stockpile operations. The government established a company called Singapore Storage & Warehouse (SSW) through Temasek Management Services, which took over the assets including warehouses and the packing plant. SSW was appointed to run the government-designated warehouses for the stockpile of rice. The rice stockpile scheme was managed by

Ministry of Trade and Industry through the Trade and Development Board, while SSW managed the physical stockpiles. The presence of National Trades Union Congress (NTUC) Fairprice Co-operative as a major stockpile participant also acted as a price setter in the local market.

DIVERSIFICATION AND VENTURING OVERSEAS

One of INTRACO's strategies for sustained growth was to diversify and have varied revenue-earning activities. This would help INTRACO's earnings during economic depressions that could wipe out a business dependent on a single product. However, its margins as well as its profits remained low ("Pointer from INTRACO", 1979). Moreover, profits from divisions that performed better were offset by those that lagged behind. INTRACO came to grips with this dilemma and reduced its commitments in areas that strained its overall profitability ("Pointer from INTRACO", 1979). However, profit projections were difficult as international trade hinged on the existing political environment.

In 1979, only a handful of contractors had ventured overseas to undertake projects abroad. One approach was banding major local construction companies to form the consortium known as the Singapore Contractors Corporation (SCC). In 1979, the SCC announced that it had secured S$85 million contract to build a palace in Jeddah, Saudi Arabia. This was the first major project won by the group against strong competition from Malaysia, South Korea and some European countries. INTRACO incorporated a new company called Singa Development Corporation with a nominal capital of S$5 million to carry out consultancy, development and contract work ("Diversification from INTRACO", 1979). This marked the first attempt by INTRACO to enter project development and consultancy in a comprehensive way.

With regard to Singa, the company was not meant to remain a wholly-owned subsidiary because its real purpose was to galvanise local contractors, architects and development consultants in a joint effort to bid for overseas construction projects (Quek, 1979).

Why did INTRACO not undertake these projects on its own? INTRACO had neither the manpower nor the required expertise to exploit the projects that its marketing abilities were able to create. However, there were several local contractors who could provide the expertise for the contracts that were won. To leverage on this, INTRACO had sent out "feelers" to the local construction industry for possible joint venture subscribers for Singa. It was reported that two local contractors as well as the government-owned International Development and Construction Corporation (Indeco) were approached (Quek, 1979).

Another INTRACO subsidiary, Orion Construction, dealt in civil, electrical engineering and ancillary services for building and other construction work ("Diversification from INTRACO", 1979). Argus Shipping Pte Ltd was 51% owned by INTRACO with an authorised capital of S$500,000 and a paid-up capital of S$10,000. Argus Shipping was incorporated on 26 October 1978. INTRACO Securities Pte Ltd was incorporated on 1 November 1978 and was 100% owned by INTRACO with an authorised paid-up capital of S$1 million.

NEW MARKETS

In 1976, Chandra Das took over the helm from Loo Siew Poh at INTRACO as its managing director. In line with the *sogo shosha* model, INTRACO devoted more resources to boost the growth of Singapore's exports overseas ("INTRACO seeks new export horizons", 1977). Chandra Das announced that while continuing to export products to major markets such as the European Economic Community (EEC) and the Eastern European bloc, INTRACO would also push for new export outlets specifically at Africa, West Asia and the Pacific Islands ("INTRACO seeks new export horizons", 1977). It was crucial to develop new markets for Singapore exporters because the demand for light consumer products was saturated in the EEC and Eastern European blocs. Moreover, the EEC wanted to achieve a higher rate of recovery and this would explain the low priority placed by the European socialist countries in their allocation of foreign exchange for light industrial consumer products. Effectively, this meant that the government of these socialist economies had starved their importers of critical foreign currency (a controlled item) to prevent them from importing light industrial consumer products. In contrast, developing countries in West Asia, Africa and the Pacific Islands had large absorption capacities for industrial goods produced by Singapore's companies.

In keeping with the *sogo shosha* model and INTRACO's role, the search for new export markets was also coupled with the desire to obtain new sources of low-cost materials supplies for Singapore's manufacturers. For example, Das pointed out that INTRACO had found chemical materials in some Eastern European countries that have never been tapped before by Singapore companies ("INTRACO seeks new export horizons", 1977). This discovery will not only improve the companies' competitiveness in overseas markets but also diversify their sources of supplies for strategic purposes.

Furthermore, INTRACO's subsidiaries were also established to form a *baseline* on which the trading company can leverage for import and export of various commodities. There was an organic symbiotic relation between INTRACO and its subsidiaries. For example, in the timber section, INTRACO operated two timber concessions in Indonesia's Kalimantan and Sumatran regions, using Singapore as a base for imports and re-exports. INTRACO's saw mill and furniture subsidiaries used these imports for its raw materials ("INTRACO seeks new export horizons", 1977). Its chairman Goh Tjoei Kok commented that INTRACO had invested in manufacturing subsidiaries and associated companies (upstream assets) because it needed the manufacturing support to complement its marketing overseas ("INTRACO on the move", 1978).

Since 1975, INTRACO's manufacturing subsidies have made a contribution to group profits even though the subsidiaries reduced group pre-tax profits by S$162,000 in the second half of 1977. In 1978, at the pre-tax level, the profit contribution was S$194,000 against a loss of S$9,000 in 1977. The drastic improvement in the performance of INTRACO's subsidiaries had been the turnaround in the profitability of Alpha Industries that manufactured ready-mixed concrete for the local and export markets. At the same time, Metrawood Pte Ltd had been increasing its sales in Australia and exploring the US market while Seasonal Garments was affected by the textile quotas set by the EEC (Sabnani, 1977). The overall profitability of INTRACO's subsidiaries were assisted by the reduced losses at Hexa Timber, which had ceased its saw milling operations and engaged in sawn timber trading. Other subsidiaries such as Rotraco Exports, which dealt in cigarettes and liquor, as well as those dealing in transport services such as container warehousing and transportation all did well and held their own ground.

INTRACO also lost several markets, but the search for new markets continued and linkages had been established in Sri Lanka, Bangladesh and West Asia (Sabnani, 1979). On the imports side, INTRACO continued to play its role as the bulk supplier of raw materials for smaller local industries. South America in the 1970s was one of the new export markets for INTRACO. In 1973, INTRACO's export to that region rose from S$33.4 million to S$156.4 million in 1975 ("INTRACO to step up tempo in South America", 1979).

VIETNAM

INTRACO and Yeo Hiap Seng established a joint venture company called Unipac Corporation Sarl in Saigon in 1973. The shareholding composition comprised 50% Vietnamese parties and 50% Singapore parties, with 25% held by INTRACO and 25% by Yeo Hiap Seng. The company had an authorised capital of about US$200,000 and would manufacture canned meat product for the South Vietnamese market. INTRACO also supplied cotton yarn to the Socialist Republic of Vietnam in 1977 to the amount of S$14.8 million. The cotton yarn was supplied by two textile mills, South Grand Textiles (Pts) Ltd and Singapore Textiles Industries Ltd (INTRACO, 1977). The outbreak of hostilities between Vietnam and Cambodia from 1975 to 1977, which culminated with Vietnam's invasion on Cambodia in 1978 to defeat the Khmer Rouge, meant a business setback for INTRACO because of the trade potential in both countries.

NORTH KOREA

INTRACO also conducted trade with isolated regimes such as North Korea. On an ad hoc basis, INTRACO traded items such as cement with the country, and it further discussed with North Korean officials about more formalised trading arrangements. In early 1978, a North Korean delegation of senior officials led by Vice Premier Kong Jin Tae visited Singapore ("INTRACO invited to send mission to North Korea", 1978). During the discussion, the North Korean vice premier promised to investigate possibilities of a more organised bilateral trade, such as through the various state corporations dealing with specific products and commodities. At the same meeting, INTRACO officials had expressed interest in importing building materials, steel items and cotton yarn from North Korea. In turn, Singapore could offer semi-processed to fully manufactured items. The sectors that could benefit from increased trade with North Korea included food and electronics ("INTRACO invited to send mission to North Korea", 1978).

CHINA

China had traditionally imported rubber and other primary products from Singapore. In the late 1970s, China bought oil rigs and drilling tools from Singapore (Foo, 1979a). In this regard, INTRACO had negotiated with the China National Light Industrial Product and Export Corporation to supply intermediate and complete electrical products to China. The supply of monochrome and colour television sets, monochrome picture tubes and cassette recorder parts to China would be secured mainly from local companies (Foo, 1979b). China's demand for picture tubes was growing following the expansion of its electronics industry. China had begun to concentrate on manufacturing 35 cm monochrome television sets and was expected to produce 1.2 million sets by the early 1980s (Foo, 1979a).

Delegations from China have also visited Singapore at the invitation of INTRACO to pursue bilateral business opportunities. For example, in 1979, China National Light Industrial Product and Export Corporation sent a delegation to Singapore to explore the possibilities of increasing bilateral trade in light industrial products between the two countries (Foo, 1979b). In January 1980, INTRACO secured a $2 million contract to sell plywood to China. The trial order was the first direct sale between both countries. The business deal was important because in previous years, all deals had to go through Hong Kong intermediaries ("INTRACO secures plywood contract from China", 1980). This was because the Chinese government had empowered a select handful of companies based in Hong Kong to manage trade with mainland China (Loh, 1986). Plywood manufacturers in Singapore also agreed to take the marketing lead from INTRACO for this sector as well as subsequent contracts. INTRACO

Picture 4.1. INTRACO Officials with Visiting Chinese Delegation. (Photo courtesy of S. Chandra Das.)

officials would also look into the possibility of extending the range of wood products that Singapore can sell to China in the future (Loh, 1986).

Then Chinese Prime Minister, Zhao Ziyang told Prime Minister Lee Kuan Yew that the city-state could become the "eyes and mouth for China's stomach", in order to help satisfy China's appetite for Western know-how. In December 1980, a consortium of eight Singapore companies signed a joint venture contract for S$40 million to establish an offshore oil base in Guangdong province ("Singapore and China: The sweet taste of co-operation", 1984). In the same year, the Singapore government also decided to let its citizens bring in domestic servants (*amahs*) from China. Singapore, conscious of geopolitics and its location between large countries such as Indonesia and Malaysia, was careful not to be seen to promote official contacts with China. Singapore asked its local papers not to print its decision on the *amahs* and announced it would not give diplomatic recognition to China until Indonesia does ("Singapore and China: The sweet taste of co-operation", 1984).

WEST ASIA

INTRACO sent a manager to Jeddah, Saudi Arabia in 1979 to establish the Jeddah display centre. The display and sales centre, set up jointly with the Singapore Manufacturer's Association (SMA), was designed to enable local manufacturers to intensify their export drive to West Asia (Foo, 1979a). INTRACO's search for new markets saw great success when it managed to establish a foothold in Iraq to secure sales of S$2 million worth of Singapore products (Tan, 1979).

Picture 4.2. INTRACO Delegation to Iraq. (Photo courtesy of S. Chandra Das.)

STATE AND CORPORATE LINKAGES

In its strategy to expand and fulfil its role as a GLC, INTRACO intensified its marketing efforts overseas particularly in West Asia, Africa, Eastern Europe, Vietnam and China. INTRACO intended to emphasise on Singapore's participation through internal buyers and inland fairs in Eastern Europe where actual orders could be concluded ("INTRACO to step up tempo in South America", 1979). At the same time, INTRACO had managed

Picture 4.3. INTRACO Delegation at Trade Fair in Iraq. (Photo courtesy of S. Chandra Das.)

to consolidate and increase its exports overseas through the sale of timber and wood products to West Asia and textile products to Vietnam ("INTRACO hit by profit setback", 1977). INTRACO had valuable subsidiaries in Vietnam and were uncertain over their future there because the Vietnamese did not officially communicate with INTRACO over its future plans.

The end of the Vietnam War brought renewed trade links with INTRACO. INTRACO Chairman Goh Tjoei Kok said, "With Vietnam, two-way trade has resumed and negotiations are in progress to place this on a regular footing. Trade with China is being developed and the company intends to build up its existing ties with the Chinese trading corporations" ("INTRACO hit by profit setback", 1977). INTRACO had hoped to play a more intensive role in China due to the country's intention to open up its market for high technology products from overseas. In May 1977, INTRACO also secured two contracts worth about S$15 million from the Vietnam National Foundries Export and Import Corporation (a Vietnamese state-owned trading company). In 1978, Singapore dispatched two fact-finding delegations to Vietnam ("INTRACO to step up tempo in South America", 1979).

The emphasis on new emerging markets was also a response to the increasing market protectionist policies of Australia, Europe and the United States ("INTRACO hit by profit setback", 1977). Australia, because of its size, poses a major challenge for INTRACO. INTRACO's regional director for Australasia and Oceania, John Hong, said that, "Because Australia is a large country, many exporters think it is an easy market. However, the size of the country is itself a major problem. The cost of distribution needs careful study in particular. Part of the solution to this is effective communications" ("INTRACO's come a long way", 1979). INTRACO has concentrated on Australia's major cities such as Sydney and Melbourne because these are centres that serviced markets in eastern Australia but also had links with Perth, Brisbane, Adelaide and Darwin. Furthermore, INTRACO's participation in the ASEAN Trade Fair in Sydney in October 1978 had enabled the company to establish more links in New South Wales, Victoria and Tasmania. One of INTRACO's subsidiaries, John White Footwear (Far East), which manufactures a range of footwear from army boots to moccasins, had problems penetrating the Australian market. John Hong added that, "What is needed to crack this market [Australia] is perseverance and marketing skill. Those who have these abilities will succeed. We have estimated the market for John White Footwear at about SGD $300,000 per year" ("INTRACO's come a long way", 1979).

For new markets such as Vietnam that were recovering from war, INTRACO's managing director Chandra Das added that he viewed INTRACO's investments there as risks, and if they were lost through being nationalised or acquired by the government, the loss had to be borne by the company. INTRACO had various interests in Vietnam, holding 22.5% to 33% in three companies — Unipac, Uniseas and Unitex ("INTRACO hit by profit setback", 1977).

In the mid-1970s, INTRACO assumed the role of representing Singapore companies in international trade events with a view towards exploring new markets. One strategy was for INTRACO to work with Singapore's trade officials. For example, INTRACO worked with the Trade Department at the Ministry of Finance to represent Singapore companies at the Lagos Trade Fair in November 1977. It was the first time that Singapore had participated in a trade fair in Nigeria. The companies that INTRACO represented at the trade fair included Swee Heng Enamelled

Wires, O Mustard and Son, Chuang's Cutlery, Lion City Shoes, John White Shoes, Red Box Light Industries, Teow Hong, Tai Onn Machinery, Hong Chuan Enterprises, Chloride Batteries, Amoy Canning, Diethelm, Cheong Heng Engineering Works, Singapore Electronic and Telecommunications and Prime Electrical Products ("INTRACO to Lagos Fair", 1977).

The SMA had argued that INTRACO and DBS Bank had failed to meet the needs of manufacturers and exporters. Since its inception in 1968, DBS was tipped by analysts to be a bank for small industrialists or would-be entrepreneurs. However, its track record several years later suggested that DBS had taken the approach to reduce altruism to a minimum and maximize profits.

INTRACO was unable to develop sufficient volume in trading because whenever it was able to build up sufficient export volume through marketing, local manufacturers contracted to supply INTRACO with the orders would step in and undercut the trading company in the next round of orders to the buyers ("A second look at DBS and INTRACO", 1979). The SMA has called for government trading companies like INTRACO that promoted the sale of Singapore-made goods overseas to enhance their networks with local manufacturers. However, two critical obstacles were hard to overcome: first, the adapted philosophy that no one owed Singapore manufacturers a living and that subsidies or featherbedding had led to shortsighted short-term gains by local manufacturers who saw no role for INTRACO in the long term. Second, the attitude of local manufacturers towards using an international trading company or a marketing intermediary such as INTRACO had to change if any product development were to come from trading concerns ("A second look at DBS and INTRACO", 1979). In its trading networks and information-gathering efforts abroad, INTRACO would have the ability to gather the demands of overseas consumers. Moreover, INTRACO would also be able to help Singapore examine the gaps in demand and supply of the international economy.

NATION'S STOCKPILER

One of INTRACO's key roles was as a major importer of commodities and raw materials for local industries. In the 1970s, two important items needed for local industries were chemicals and copra. INTRACO also acted as a local agent for overseas manufacturers and suppliers. In 1978, INTRACO supplied nearly 90% of the PVC resin requirements for the domestic market (Sabnani, 1979).

At the time, INTRACO was consolidating its position as a major importer of commodities and raw materials for local industries and had become the largest importer of copra, PVC resins and caustic soda in Singapore. The company also supplied local companies with asbestos, non-ferrous metal, paper and other industrial raw materials ("INTRACO makes headway", 1979). By the end of the decade in the1970s, INTRACO had become a diversified trading and manufacturing enterprise with an annual turnover of S$100 million. To expand its role beyond that of a trade intermediary, INTRACO had established seven subsidiaries and nine associated companies ("INTRACO's come a long way", 1979). Chandra Das and his team of senior executives were building the foundations of a Singapore *sogo shosha*, but arguably, to the outsider, the company began to look too diversified and without focus. There should have been greater conviction by the board of directors and executive committee to support INTRACO in this strategic planning.

Table 4.2 shows profits for INTRACO at the company and group levels from 1972 to 1979. The results show that INTRACO's profits were steadily increasing at both levels.

During critical junctures in Singapore's economic growth, INTRACO had been depended upon to assist local industries because of unplanned

Table 4.2. Profits for INTRACO at Company and Group Level, 1972–1979 (S$'000).

	1972	**1973**	**1974**	**1975**	**1976**	**1977**	**1978**	**1979**
Company								
Profits before taxation	1,214	3,613	4,074	2,327	3,088	3,080	3,211	4,246
Profits after taxation	764	2,163	2,374	1,477	1,803	2,080	2,311	2,696
Group								
Profits before taxation	1,274	3,607	4,237	1,913	2,849	2,907	4,176	5,561
Profits after taxation	772	2,059	2,549	1,111	1,532	1,912	2,999	3,405

Source: INTRACO annual reports.

external events. For example, in 1973, Singapore suffered from a shortage of timber because Malaysia banned export of its timber ("INTRACO brings in Indon timber to relieve shortage", 1973). INTRACO had two Indonesian timber concessions and planned to import 45,000 cubic metres of logs a month from these concessions from local sawmills and plywood factories in East Kalimantan and Sumatra through its two subsidiaries Forest Development Pte Ltd and Goodwin Timbers Pte Ltd, respectively. Originally, timber from these concessions was exported to the Japanese market but supplies were diverted to Singapore due to the shortage. While INTRACO managed to secure timber supplies, there were other problems such as contracting tugboats to bring in regular shipment of logs. As a result, INTRACO hired about a dozen barges and tugboats from the Port of Singapore Authority (PSA) to ship in about 30,000 to 40,000 logs a month from its 400,000-acre concession in Sumatra (Mohan, 1972). INTRACO signed a charter contract with the PSA to use its tugboats and barges to ship the logs into Singapore (Mohan, 1972). In June 1978, INTRACO sent a senior management team to Sumatra to reorganise and oversee the operations of two timber concessions in Medan and Aceh.

TOWARDS THE 1980s

By 1979, INTRACO had an annual turnover of S$120 million and was a diversified group of companies with more than 20 companies in shipping, furniture, garment manufacturing, timber extraction and trading. The company maintained overseas representative offices in Europe, West Asia and Australasia ("Diversification from INTRACO", 1979). INTRACO had also secured S$2.4 million worth of orders from Hungary for ready-made garments. The orders came through INTRACO's participation in the Budapest International Autumn Fair on 14 September 1979 ("INTRACO secures $2.4 m orders", 1979). There was great demand among Hungarians for Singapore-made summer clothing. A delegation from the Hungarian Importing Company, a state-owned organisation had also visited Singapore to explore ways to boost bilateral trade linkages ("INTRACO secures $2.4 m orders", 1979).

INTRACO was preparing for a role in oil trading by purchasing a stake of about 10% in a huge storage terminal on Pulau Sebarok, an island in the south of Singapore costing more than S$100 million and developed by

Picture 4.4. INTRACO Officials at Trade Fair. (Photo courtesy of S. Chandra Das.)

Picture 4.5. INTRACO Officials at Trade Fair. (Photo courtesy of S. Chandra Das.)

Dutch company Van Ommeren (Lim and Foo, 1980). The other partner was the PSA with 35% while Van Ommeren held 55%. The terminal is to be used for storing refined petrochemical products, edible oils, chemicals and gases. Singapore aimed to be distribution centre for the fast expanding oil-trading activity in the region (Lim and Foo, 1980). The terminal would also be used as a warehouse for trading companies handling both spot and contract oil deals. Singapore was also keen to acquire oil supplies on a government-to-government basis from Iraq. Iraq as a socialist state also preferred barter trading, and INTRACO would be the logical choice to act on behalf of the government (Lim and Foo, 1980).

INTRACO was interested in marketing Singapore-made petrochemicals from the Ayer Merbau complex. INTRACO's managing director Chandra Das intended to market Singapore-produced petrochemicals primarily in the ASEAN region as well as in emerging markets such as China (Lim, 1980). In addition, INTRACO could also market petrochemicals in other socialist countries. At the time, INTRACO's experience in

Picture 4.6. INTRACO and Japanese Partners (Daimei). (Photo courtesy of S. Chandra Das.)

petrochemicals marketing had been in the imports of PVC resins, low- and high-density polyethylene and plastic materials for factories and plastics manufacturers.

NGO LINKAGES

In the 1970s, increasing numbers of refugees known as the boat people were leaving Vietnam and Cambodia. Singapore became an important staging area for various non-governmental organisations (NGOs) because of its location and logistical capabilities. The NGOs had sought assistance from Singapore's Ministry of Foreign Affairs (MFA) to link them up with suitable suppliers for food rations that needed to be purchased and shipped overseas. MFA linked these NGOs such as Oxfam and World Vision to INTRACO. The NGOs needed to purchase and ship food supplies to Vietnam after the fall of Saigon in 1975 and in 1979 to Cambodia that was devastated by the genocide caused by the Khmer Rouge. Although traders in Singapore made good profits assisting various NGOs, INTRACO undertook the role of supplier not for profit but because it was called to do so by the government. Then managing director of INTRACO, Chandra Das instructed his INTRACO team not to overcharge the NGOs using their services because it was for a humanitarian cause and Singapore's reputation was at stake.[2] Das and his team also went to meet the Oxfam executives at their headquarters in Oxford in the United Kingdom to discuss plans on the refugee problem. INTRACO further arranged for the transportation of the food aid to Cambodia. After the fall of Saigon, when the boat people came to Singapore waters, they were housed in refugee camps on Kallang Island. INTRACO was contracted by World Vision to acquire and deliver mobile toilets to the refugee camp.[3]

CESS TAX

The CESS tax imposed on Singapore companies trading with Socialist countries was administered by INTRACO. CESS from imports ranged

[2] Interview with former INTRACO senior executive, PY, 1 July 2011.
[3] *Ibid.*

from 0.2% of CIF (cost, insurance and freight) values, depending on the item imported. Apart from the cost of the inconvenience, local traders were also unhappy that the CESS was collected on the government's behalf by INTRACO Ltd (Mehta and Lee, 1992). Although traders could claim a refund of the CESS if the goods were re-exported, seeking reimbursement was seldom easy. Traders were also required to stipulate in advance the name of the transshipment vessel. As INTRACO was also a competitor, a trader said, "When we fill up the papers at INTRACO, we are disclosing trade information to them. Why should we do that?"(Mehta and Lee, 1992). Moreover, it was not always easy to claim the refund. For example, Abedeen Tyebally of Bombay Trading said he had waited three months to receive a refund of more than S$10,000 for importing raw cashew nuts which were re-exported (Mehta and Lee, 1992).

Nonetheless, the 1970s saw great promise for INTRACO to be a Singapore *sogo shosha*. However, it could also be argued that the objective to develop INTRACO into a trading organisation along the lines of a Japanese trading organisation had failed despite the company's connections and financial reserves. Why did INTRACO fail to live up to its expectations? To a large extent, the company could in its defence explain that whenever it managed to build up sufficient export volume through diligent marketing, the wily local contractors that supplied the INTRACO orders would step in and undercut the trading company from the next round of orders ("A second look at DBS and INTRACO", 1979).

Despite problems in the external environment and internal issues such as the CESS tax, INTRACO had a critical role to play in the growth of the Singapore economy. This "window" of opportunity was sadly missed by the company and the state to support INTRACO's development to be a *sogo shosha*. The following chapter will cover INTRACO's development from 1980 to 1990. It will encompass the end of the Cold War and changing global conditions that adversely impacted INTRACO's businesses. This period also questioned the continued relevance of INTRACO in business and as a GLC.

CHAPTER 5

INTERNATIONALISATION AND "ROUGH WATERS" — 1980s TO 1990

EXPLORING EMERGING MARKETS

While the 1960s and 1970s saw the expansion of government-linked companies (GLCs) including INTRACO and the visible hand of the government in economic development, the mid-1980s saw the government encouraging more entrepreneurship from the corporate sector and a reduced role for GLCs in the domestic economy. The principal roles of the GLCs then were to fill strategic gaps in the economy. These gaps occurred because the sectors in question were not attractive enough to international investments, were too much of a public good or too strategic to turn to a foreign enterprise (Huff, 1995, p. 1429). The strategy of divesting government shares in GLCs to nurture privatisation increased in pace from the mid-1980s onwards (Sikorski, 1989, p. 82). One of the criticisms levelled at INTRACO was its lack of focus regarding its trading interests due to its involvement in a diverse array of businesses. This criticism highlights the lack of understanding of observers, including policy makers, its board of directors and its executive committee, regarding the trading business and role of the *sogo shosha* in the Japanese economy.

This chapter examines the core areas of INTRACO's business activities, such as providing materials and services for infrastructure development, commodities trading and diversification into new business ventures by acquisitions. Global events also influenced INTRACO's role and had an impact on its businesses; these included the end of the Cold War in the late

1990s and dissolution of the Soviet Bloc, forming Russia and the CIS states. The establishment of diplomatic relations with China in the early 1990s spelt the eventual redundancy for the CESS tax and created more competition from local traders. Other global events that affected INTRACO's businesses were the First Gulf War in the Middle East and Gulf states as well as the Balkans War in the former Yugoslavia.

One of the key strategies for the long-term survival of trading firms depended on their ability to create new and diverse opportunities and to maintain a widely dispersed network of businesses (Larke and Davies, 2007, p. 377). From the example of the *sogo shosha*, this network is highly dynamic and diverse, consisting of a large variety of skills and business fields. It has been argued that with more sophisticated and differentiated goods that require trade services, brand name development and after-sales service would marginalise the role of the *sogo shosha*. However, since the 1990s, the *shosha* have expanded their business profile beyond the role of government trading companies and into more direct roles within the Japanese market. The inability of INTRACO to expand their activities in the domestic economy because of concerns from local businesses further curtailed their growth. In this regard, perhaps the local business communities were not as supportive as their counterparts were of the *shosha* in Japan. While local companies argued that INTRACO should be expanding its activities outside of Singapore and reducing its role in the domestic market, they were shown to have benefitted from INTRACO's exploration of new markets and bulk purchase of raw materials for local manufacturers.

INTRACO entered the 1980s with more than 12 years of operating in the international economy. It had accumulated a range of activities and expertise from the production of garments, metal roofing sheets, footwear, knock-down furniture, marketing of edible oils, engineering products and others. However, INTRACO remained primarily a trading company and its main role was to explore new export markets for Singapore's manufacturers ("Going places", 1980). Singapore's three major trading partners, Japan, Europe and the United States were facing slow economic growth. However, INTRACO was not unduly worried about the bleak economic projections for the developed economies ("INTRACO not worried by bleak reports", 1980). This was because

INTRACO had focused on establishing links with developing countries that were unhindered by various protectionist measures found in developed countries ("Going places", 1980). This new focus in 1980 was seen when INTRACO deployed personnel overseas to strengthen its operations abroad. This focus can be seen when its chairman Goh Tjoei Kok announced in 1980 that, to "strengthen [its] overseas operations, [INTRACO] deployed a manager to start up a representative office in Sri Lanka and added another manager to [its] office in Medan" ("INTRACO not worried by bleak reports", 1980).

West Asia was another key region for INTRACO to explore. INTRACO had established a representative office in Saudi Arabia manned by a Singaporean. This provided the thrust and support to explore more business opportunities in the Middle East ("INTRACO to set up Saudi office later this year", 1980). INTRACO had participated actively in the Baghdad International Fair among 60 other countries. At the fair, INTRACO had reserved more than 90 m^2 of exhibition space for Singapore manufacturers

Picture 5.1. INTRACO Delegation in Iraq. (Photo courtesy of S. Chandra Das.)

to promote their products ("INTRACO poised for bigger role", 1980). The company's strength that enabled it to penetrate the Iraqi market was the support that it received from the Singapore government and its track record. With regard to Iraq, INTRACO had always been punctual in delivering its goods to fulfil contract schedules. Lam Peck Heng, INTRACO's planning and development manager had said, "For some countries, we ship first and worry about payment later", to establish good trading relations ("INTRACO poised for bigger role", 1980). Moreover, socialist countries like Iraq preferred to deal with their counterparts in state-owned organisations ("INTRACO poised for bigger role", 1980).

ORGANISATIONAL EXPANSION

INTRACO had worked with the Singapore government in export promotion with advanced teams exploring the West Asian region and specific economies like Iraq and Saudi Arabia. The government was also involved in a human resource programme with INTRACO by providing staff such as a senior official from the Department of Trade who was seconded to INTRACO for the establishment of the Jeddah office (Lim, 1980). Venturing into new markets, INTRACO had restructured and brought in more personnel, which was necessary for the company to "take-off" and expand (Lim, 1980). INTRACO had restructured its manpower base through deleting the posts of regional directors and creating three new general manager positions in trading, manufacturing and investment and business development ("INTRACO recruits new execs in expansion drive", 1980). This was meant to provide senior executives with more operational knowledge of their respective departments and the products they were handling. For example, Charlie Phua was promoted to the post of general manager for trading; Gopinath Pillai was appointed general manager for manufacturing and investments; and Rex Shelley was appointed as general manager for business development ("INTRACO recruits new execs in expansion drive", 1980). Interestingly, in terms of linkages between the company and the government, senior INTRACO executives also held concurrent designations in government and other institutions. For example, Rex Shelley was a member of the Public Services Commission (PSC).

Gopinath Pillai was appointed as the head of the products committee in the Singapore Manufacturers Association (SMA), and Chandra Das stood in the general elections as a People's Action Party (PAP) candidate ("INTRACO recruits new execs in expansion drive", 1980).

In order to strengthen its financial position so as to wean the company off government financial support, in 1981, INTRACO had raised S$60 million through a one-for-one new rights issue at S$4 per share. The issue was made more attractive for potential shareholders with a bonus issue of one for four (Ong, 1981). The additional funding was meant to develop an office building, warehouses and key projects such as buying a 10% stake in the S$100 million Pulau Sebarok oil storage terminal (Ong, 1981). This could lead to INTRACO buying oil from the spot market (Lim, 1980). The projects were for the long-term benefit of the company and were expected to contribute to shareholder's dividends only from 1985 (Lim, 1981a).

However, it was difficult for the company to sever links with the state as the government, through Temasek Holdings Ltd, had undertaken to subscribe for its full entitlement share of INTRACO's one-for-one rights of 15 million shares. Temasek Holdings was a major shareholder of INTRACO with 3.2 million shares. With the offer, Temasek's stake was increased to 4 million shares, then 8 million shares after the rights issue (Lim, 1981a). The Development Bank of Singapore (DBS) underwrote the remaining 11 million share rights. In addition, DBS was also managing the rights issue, which raised S$59.56 million after deducting underwriting commission and relevant expenses.

Seeking greater financial independence and resources, INTRACO was preparing to purchase a 35% stake in the Far Eastern Bank of Singapore, but the government, especially the financial authorities, were not keen on the idea because of the risks involved ("South-east Asians on the move", 1983). At the time, INTRACO's strategy was similar to other trading houses in the region. Southeast Asia's biggest companies promoted by autocratic governments had diversified rapidly and were beginning to outgrow their home markets ("South-east Asians on the move", 1983). Essentially, it was a race between INTRACO and its regional competitors to dominate trading and related activities in the region. For example, the family-owned Liem group in Indonesia wanted to diversify abroad and bought a company in Hong Kong in 1982 to establish First Pacific Holdings. Through First Pacific Holdings, the Liem group acquired the Hibernia Bank, which was the 12th largest bank in California, for US$75 million; and a Dutch trading company called Hagemeyer for US$19 million. The Liem family aimed to acquire the same strengths as the *sogo shosha* by combining credit and trading skills; Hagemeyer was already importing large quantities of Indonesian coffee into the United States and Hibernia would be able to finance the trade. Moreover, Hibernia was also handling the wheat imports to Indonesia worth US$330 million at the time and earning US$2 million as fees ("South-east Asians on the move", 1983).

Similar to the Liem group of companies, Malayan United Industries had used a Hong Kong company called Cesuco Trading to expand its activities overseas. Malayan United Industries was one of the five largest Malayan companies in market capitalisation. It bought a 20% share of a Western Australian food company called Peters and established a property and trading firm in Vancouver, Canada. However, some regional company expansions had gone badly. The Construction and Development Corporation of the Philippines was one example. The company was too dependent on the Philippine economy and expanded overseas too quickly, especially in the Middle East, and raked up bank debts of US$795 million. The Philippine government had to take over the company and manage its debts ("South-east Asians on the move", 1983).

So why did INTRACO expand internationally? INTRACO's managing director Chandra Das explained that it was necessary to develop marketing outlets in the Southeast Asian region because the Singapore market was relatively small. For example, the domestic market only absorbed about 20% of the PVC imported from Eastern Europe. INTRACO's international franchise could not be successful if they had depended only on the local market. With markets in the US and Western Europe already saturated, both peninsular and East Malaysia came under closer scrutiny by INTRACO for trading and business opportunities (Lim, 1981b). INTRACO saw Malaysia not only as a hinterland for source materials but as a rich export market as well. Malaysia was a major exporter of traditional items like palm oil and timber. While a traditional trading partner, Malaysia, with its strong growth, had improved its prospects as a sales outlet for INTRACO (Lim, 1981b).

ANGOLA DIAMOND MINES

INTRACO also ventured further afield for business opportunities. For example, in 1984, INTRACO was involved in the maintenance and repair of all the earth-moving equipment, cranes, drills, generators, haulers and trucks for Diamang, a diamond mining company in Angola. At the time, in terms of personnel and fleet size, it was probably the biggest maintenance contract of its kind in the world. INTRACO employed 175 of its own expatriate technicians in Luanda Norte, Angola, as well as supervised another 50 expatriates and 600 Angolans employed by Diamang. INTRACO was responsible for the repair and maintenance of a 460-item caterpillar fleet including haul trucks, wheel-type loaders, bulldozers and other equipment. INTRACO also carried out the reconstruction of the bridge over the River Cuilo in May 1983 over a span of three weeks. The bridge had been sabotaged by rebels in December 1982 and was a vital road network to the diamond areas (Helmore, 1984).

MALDIVES

As part of its expansion into new markets, INTRACO formed a trading joint venture company with the Maldivian government called Simalco Enterprises in 1981. Simalco began to export pre-fabricated chalets from Singapore to the Maldives. Simalco was 51% owned by INTRACO and 49% owned by the Maldivian government (Lim, 1981b). Singapore also accounted for more than half the products such as fruit, vegetables, canned foods, oil products and wheat flour imported by the Maldives each year (Koh, 1985). INTRACO had also planned to lease an entire island in the Maldives to develop a modern tourist resort. Together with Singapore Airlines and perhaps a Maldivian partner, the group aimed to develop a modern hotel with a restaurant and swimming pool. They wanted to attract high-spending tourists from South-east Asia and Japan. Singapore Airlines had placed the Maldives as part of its European routes in March 1984.

CHINESE PROVINCES

In 1981, INTRACO's managing director Chandra Das commented that there was huge potential in the Chinese market. Following the Chinese government's policy of decentralisation and allowing the provinces more flexibility to conduct their economic activities, this has enabled foreign investors and businesses to deal directly with the provincial authorities (Lim, 1981b). In China, INTRACO had gone a step further to establish trade relations by concluding trade pacts with specific provinces. In January 1981, INTRACO signed an agreement with the Guangdong provincial government to purchase 8,000 to 10,000 pieces of fine Chinese handicrafts. These ceramics would be sourced from the Nanchang province, famous as the home of the best ceramics and antique pottery in China (Lim, 1981b).

At the time, exports to China included industrial products such as television tubes, time pieces, plywood and chemicals for Chinese industries. However, INTRACO was keen to emphasise that it would not "rob" importers of China-made goods of their business ("INTRACO: Pact will not hit existing importers", 1981). This provision was included in the agreement and INTRACO's assistant general manager Lam Peck Heng had reassured local importers that they need not worry about competition from the company, as there were plenty of opportunities for trading with China ("INTRACO: Pact will not hit existing importers", 1981). The Chinese were keen on purchasing timber logs, plywood, PVC compounds for cables, pipes, bottles and engineering machinery that were made in Singapore. In return, INTRACO was interested in purchasing from Guangdong province, spices, dried goods, feed materials, frozen fish, canned food and raw and semi-finished materials for the manufacture of pharmaceutical products, building materials, steel products, textile and engineering items ("INTRACO: Pact will not hit existing importers", 1981).

In April 1981, INTRACO signed a trade agreement with Fujian province in China (Hsung, 1981). This opened the possibility of direct negotiations between INTRACO and trading corporations in Fujian. INTRACO was interested in marketing a wide range of industrial and consumer products from Fujian province. A Fujian economic delegation headed by its deputy governor Guo Chao had visited INTRACO officials in Singapore. The Fujian delegation was interested in promoting joint venture and trade with local entrepreneurs. An INTRACO official emphasised that while INTRACO wanted to market more Chinese products, it would not encroach on product lines being handled by local agents. There were no specific mechanics on how INTRACO was supposed to avoid imported product lines already handled by local agents; these were verbal assurances mentioned by INTRACO's senior executives. It was also difficult for local agents to develop any business links with INTRACO because of the CESS. INTRACO as the agency that manages the CESS was privy to information on all the goods imported by local agents from China.

The Fujian agreement would also create more diversity to its supply lines and promote the export of goods from Singapore to Fujian province and in particular electronic goods. The proposed agreement fell within INTRACO's strategic aim to diversify its sources of supply (Hsung, 1981).

MID-1980S — SHRINKING ECONOMY?

The recession of 1985 saw the economy shrink by 1.8% for the first time in decades. In 1985, Singapore plunged into its first recession. The minister responsible for the economy, Dr Tony Tan, had joined the Cabinet in 1980, and he was the Minister for Trade & Industry (1981–1986) as well as Minister for Finance (1983–1985). The PAP government attempted a bold restructuring of the Singapore economy in the early 1980s, often referred to as its Second Industrial Revolution. This was to move the economy into skill- and capital-intensive industries, and produce high value-added goods. One of the means to achieve it was through the use of National Wages Council (NWC) as a means of raising wage rates well ahead of productivity so as to force firms to upgrade and to move "upmarket". The Singapore economy started to slow significantly after the first quarter of 1984 and recorded a negative 10.1% year-on-year growth in the second quarter of 1985, before coming out of the recession in the first quarter of 1986.

Overall, real GDP declined by 1.7% in 1985. While external factors had a role to play, internal events were key in explaining the causes of the recession. The most important of these, the rise in unit labour costs, can be linked directly to the policies of the Second Industrial Revolution. Labour costs ran far ahead of productivity, and as a result, Singapore lost its international competitiveness significantly against its Asian Tiger peers — Taiwan, South Korea and Hong Kong. In March 1985, Dr Tony Tan announced the creation of an Economic Committee to study the causes of the recession and identify policy remedies. The committee was chaired by newcomer Brigadier-General Lee Hsien Loong, who had only been appointed as Minister of State in the Ministry of Trade and Industry in January 1985, right after the December 1984 election. The Economic Committee completed its report one year later, and its policy recommendations included reducing Central Provident Fund (CPF) contributions, wage restraint, reduction in tax rates, the divestment of GLCs and the promotion of services sector, etc. In February 1986, BG Lee Hsien Loong was appointed Acting Minister for Trade and Industry, replacing his predecessor, Dr Tony Tan, who had also relinquished the Finance Ministry portfolio, returned to the Education Ministry.

Policy makers realised that MNC-led growth was not sufficient for the economy's overall growth (Zutshi and Gibbons, 1998, p. 230), and that local entrepreneurship, technological development and internationalisation had to be nurtured. The government established the Economic Committee Report for the Ministry of Trade and Industry and the Public Sector Divestment Committee (PSDC) in 1987. At the operational level, GLCs were allowed to compete with one another in the domestic economy. The internal and accountability structure were further reformed with multi-tiered subsidiaries and performance bonuses to encourage entrepreneurial activities (Zutshi and Gibbons, 1998, p. 230). How are the GLCs linked to the state? Due to the various legal acts that govern the establishment of statutory boards and corporations, the communication links between the GLCs and government occurred both at the formal and informal levels.

In the late 1980s, INTRACO also adopted a "country approach" for its trading business by developing an overseas presence in countries which it had traded with such as Vietnam and China. Nonetheless, INTRACO also explored business opportunities elsewhere in emerging economies and had explored business opportunities in exotic locations like Africa, such as the diamond mines of Angola. Some of the areas of INTRACO's business interests included equipment procurement and contract administration. Its other business interests included power supply generation and transmission and distribution equipment. Some of its loss-making ventures included its car dealerships (for brands such as Holden, Lada and Rover), and commodities trading and business links with Teledata. INTRACO continued to explore new emerging markets like Myanmar and Vietnam.

LEMON DEALS

INTRACO also fell victim to business scams or more commonly called "lemon deals" among businessmen. For example in 1987, INTRACO was involved in a bogus plywood deal that cost the company S$10 million in losses (Yong, 1990a, b). In the scam, INTRACO opened a letter of credit in favour of an Indonesian firm to pay for the plywood that it had ordered from Indonesia for its clients in China. However, the plywood was never delivered. It took the Singapore government three years to put INTRACO's house in order after this incident. The management shake-up was settled with the appointment of Tien Sin Cheong, a former senior vice-president of Seagate Technology, as INTRACO's new managing director in 1987. INTRACO reviewed its "overseeing role", and strengthened its management procedures. INTRACO chairman Hwang Peng Yuan said that "lessons learned from the plywood supply failure has been put to use" ("INTRACO beefs up management procedures after last year's fraud incident", 1988). INTRACO also learnt valuable lessons in the undertaking of loss-making investments such as Multi-pak and Everbloom Mushroom. Ultimately, INTRACO was still a profitable and cash-rich company ("UIC chief appointed to board of INTRACO", 1986).

Unfortunately, INTRACO's profitability and image was further dented by the stock market. During the 1986–1987 "bull" run on the market, INTRACO's share price hit a peak of S$4.60 but this was knocked down to a low of S$1.58 during the October 1987 stock market crash.

DIVESTING GLCS

While GLCs have been a major element in Singapore's economic development, two main criticisms have been levelled at them. The first is that GLCs perform better than the companies in the private sector because their institutional ties with the government give them unique access to funds, tenders and opportunities, which arguably close off large areas of the economy and stifle entrepreneurship. The second criticism is that GLCs perform worse than the private companies because their management teams comprise largely of civil servants who lack entrepreneurial abilities, and investments may be politically rather than commercially motivated (Tan, 2004). Arguably, there are various ways in which GLCs could receive financial assistance from the government such as government loan guarantees, concessional interest rates and generous payment terms and periods (Tan, 2004).

In 1986, the PSDC had recommended a policy of controlled dynamism under which GLCs are charged with the responsibility of getting ready for privatisation as soon as possible and choosing the timing that is most advantageous to them. Ironically, Hwang Peng Yuan who was to become chairman of the board of directors at INTRACO was a member of the PSDC and identified INTRACO as one of the GLCs to be totally privatised (De Silva, 1987).

Why was INTRACO a non-core GLC? If Temasek had deemed INTRACO as a non-core GLC, it could have divested its shares completely in the company when United Industrial Corporation (UIC) made a takeover bid for INTRACO in 1986 (Sikorski, 1989, p. 80). The Divestment Committee Report stated that "Divestments should not be rushed at the expense of value that maybe realised. Thus, shares will not be disposed of unless the selling authority or the Minister for Finance is satisfied with the price" (Ministry of Trade and Industry, 1987).

FAILED "TAKEOVER" OF INTRACO

It could also be argued that Temasek was unable to divest all its interests in INTRACO because the company needed government support to continue its overseas ventures, especially those with China (Lim, 1988). INTRACO chairman Hwang Peng Yuan commented that the government would want to keep the company as a state trading enterprise (STE) due to its relations with other state-owned companies in Eastern Europe and China. UIC had sought to acquire Temasek's stake in INTRACO (26.7%) in late 1985 ("INTRACO and UIC steal the limelight", 1986). By being the second largest shareholder with 17.8% in INTRACO, UIC requested for a seat on the board of directors at INTRACO. Subsequently, the chairman of UIC Dennis Lee Kim Yew (brother of then Prime Minister Lee Kuan Yew) was appointed to the board of directors at INTRACO ("UIC chief appointed to board of INTRACO", 1986). This gave rise to speculation that UIC had sensed that INTRACO was vulnerable after the resignation of its managing director Chandra Das and the exodus of its senior management, about 15 in all (Ong, 1985). However, the offered price for INTRACO at S$3.20 was not sufficient and the deal fell through. The exodus of INTRACO's senior management to join rival trading companies such as Haw Par Trading and Ambassador Holding Limited increased the uncertainty over the future of INTRACO (Cheng, 1986a). The international press also speculated that since Temasek was a shareholder in both the companies, the response of the Singapore government was likely to be the determining factor (Sikorski, 1989, p. 80). Table 5.1 shows the largest shareholders of INTRACO at the end of 1980. Chart 5.1 (in the Annex) shows the Organisational Chart at INTRACO. Temasek divested itself of UIC in 1986.

What was the significant trend in the pricing of shares in the mid- to late 1980s? Saunders and Lim noted that in the Singapore IPO market in the 1980s, significant amounts of under-pricing existed and, on average, the degree of under-pricing was greater than that observed in more developed equity markets such as the United Kingdom (Saunders and Lim, 1990, p. 297). They argued that there were several reasons for under-pricing. These included huge oversubscription and a rationing system employed for Singapore IPOs; the potential monopoly enjoyed by commercial banks and commercial bank–merchant conglomerate underwriters over new issuing firms; issuers' concerns about future access to the equity market for secondary offerings as well as concerns over due diligence and potential future legal and reputational liabilities (Saunders and Lim, 1990, p. 297).

Reportedly, a source at INTRACO had said that the company lost its insulating layer when its general manager Chandra Das left the group in

Table 5.1. Largest Shareholders of INTRACO in 1980.

Name	No. of shares	% of shareholding
Temasek Holdings (Pte) Ltd	3,202,000	26.68
Thye Heng (How Kee) Sdn Bhd	1,747,000	14.56
DBS Nominees (Pte) Ltd	1,531,500	12.76
National Iron & Steel Mills Ltd	240,000	2.00

Source: INTRACO annual report (1981).

1986, and added, "some of them we should never have lost" ("Tough tests ahead for INTRACO after management exodus", 1986). After nine years as managing director of INTRACO, Chandra Das resigned. He explained that public criticism of INTRACO was unfounded. The role of GLCs in the domestic economy was of great concern and the perception among local companies was that INTRACO had extended its tentacles into a variety of trading and manufacturing activities. He was surprised that the role of GLCs had surfaced again for discussions. Of INTRACO, Das said "[it] has been a convenient 'whipping boy' and there was no truth in suggestions that INTRACO had an adverse impact on many small Singapore traders and entrepreneurs" ("INTRACO's outgoing MD confident of company's prospects", 1986). The only group that had been affected was the rice traders who had been responsible for an inefficient supply and distribution network. Das said INTRACO had done the public a service by taking over the rice trade. He commented, "Why can't I go to China?", and added that he had taken eight Singapore companies with INTRACO when he first signed a joint venture development agreement for the Chiwan supply base in China ("INTRACO's outgoing MD confident of company's prospects", 1986). Das also commented that INTRACO had the right to compete in the local market. For example, INTRACO put in a bid and competed with other companies to supply floor tiles to the Housing Development Board (HDB). INTRACO was able to secure the supply contract based on their competitive bid. When Chandra Das resigned, general manager Charlie Phua was appointed as acting managing director while a search was made for a new managing director. Charlie Phua was not offered the top management post permanently and subsequently resigned, which meant that INTRACO had lost all of its pioneering management team (Foo, 1986).

How would owners maintain links with GLCs? One way would be the appointment of a competent board of directors who, on behalf of the owners, are responsible for assisting and monitoring the management team (Anwar and Sam, 2006, p. 42). INTRACO's board of directors had shown its displeasure over the company's poor performance, which some analysts had said was more the result of the economic recession rather than management ineptitude (Ong, 1985). The recession of the mid-1980s was a turning point for Singapore and had caused significant economic hardship (Sabhlok, 2001). A rise in protectionism in several countries, a decline in demand for raw materials and a fall in commodity prices had an adverse impact on trading companies like INTRACO. However, INTRACO's problem also appeared to be internal because it did not have a well-defined corporate image and its aggressiveness in the local market had led to legal entanglements (Cheng, 1986a). INTRACO's original brief was to develop Singapore's markets overseas and not encroach on the domestic economy. The INTRACO board's displeasure was at the heart of a long-drawn debate between the management and directors (Ong, 1985). Observers had also commented that INTRACO did not have a well-defined corporate image. The company had extended itself into a variety of activities, from selling condoms to cement. Its aggressiveness had also led to several legal entanglements and had been the target of complaints by companies in the private sector. These companies had protested that INTRACO posed unfair competition for their businesses (Ong, 1985).

The issue of rice trading was a sensitive topic because of INTRACO's role in breaking the rice monopoly among traders in Singapore. With regard to rice imported from Thailand, INTRACO as the government's agent bought rice in conjunction with the Trade and Development Board (TDB) on a government-to-government basis ("INTRACO denies any part in rice resale", 1980). One of the key conditions of the government-to-government contract with Thailand was that the rice should not be re-exported. In 1980, INTRACO and the Singapore government were alleged to have taken part in the reselling of 10,000 tonnes of Thai rice to Iran. This was denied by INTRACO and the Singapore government who clarified that the rice sale to Iran was negotiated entirely by the Singapore rice importers from their own stocks ("INTRACO denies any part in rice resale", 1980).

Then outgoing INTRACO managing director Chandra Das had said that the company had "been a convenient 'whipping boy'", and there was no truth to the allegations that INTRACO had adversely impacted on small Singapore traders and entrepreneurs ("INTRACO's outgoing MD confident of company's prospects", 1986). INTRACO also had a near monopoly in the import of rice. As a reaction to INTRACO's near monopoly on rice — the company had imported 43,000 tonnes of rice for the local market and maintained its position as the government's rice stockpile agent — the government put an end to this by liberalising rice import licenses in 1974. In 1986, the government liberalised rice import licenses

Picture 5.2. Haw Par Trading Joint Venture with Impexmetal (Poland). (Photo courtesy of S. Chandra Das.)

and INTRACO lost its near monopoly. In order to compensate for the lost earnings, INTRACO bought and sold miscellaneous products (Yong, 1990a, b). The majority of INTRACO's senior executives who had resigned went to work at rival trading company, Haw Par Trading, including Charlie Phua, while some went to work for Windmills Trading.

INTRACO'S NEW MANAGEMENT TEAM

INTRACO posted lower group turnover of S$177.27 million in 1986, down from S$215.51 million in 1985 ("Buoyant associates help shore up INTRACO's earnings", 1986). The recruitment process to replace the senior managers was problematic because there was a scarcity of marketers and traders. An observer had commented that INTRACO was recruiting new staff to fill the void created "indirectly" (Cheng, 1986a).

In 1987, newly appointed INTRACO CEO Chin Teck Huat then announced the temporary appointments of the two senior personnel from the DBS. This was part of an ongoing drive by the company to streamline and restructure its operations (Cheng, 1986b). DBS, another GLC that owns a significant minority stake in INTRACO, had seconded its two senior executives to shore up the management team at INTRACO. The DBS senior executives were Chow Kok Kee from DBS Bank and Ms Lim Joke Mui from DBS Land ("Top management changes at INTRACO", 1987).

CEO Chin Teck Huat faced the twin challenges of corporate growth and managing and moulding a mixed team of older and wiser senior and more junior executives, to rebuild INTRACO and prepare the company to handle new businesses ("DBS will help INTRACO look for new business", 1986). Chow Kok Kee, who was vice-president of corporate banking, planning and support at DBS, assumed the role of INTRACO's corporate planner. He had commented that "one of my duties will be to identify new businesses and targets" and also help in the upgrading of the company's management information systems ("DBS will help INTRACO look for new business", 1986). Lim Joke Mui was assistant general manager of finance, administration, engineering and property at DBS Land (a subsidiary of the banking group). She assumed the financial controller and company secretary position at INTRACO ("DBS will help INTRACO look for new business", 1986). A former senior executive of INTRACO who was seconded to stabilize the company after the mass exodus had said that these two DBS employees were reluctant to remain in INTRACO for long and were merely there to assist in shoring it up (Interview with former INTRACO executive, 7 July 2011). When approached for an interview by the writer, Chow declined and Lim did not reply to the writer's inquiry via email.

When the UIC takeover bid for INTRACO took place, INTRACO appointed merchant bank Wardley Limited as its adviser, while Morgan Greenfell (Asia) represented UIC and Baring Brothers (Asia) advised Temasek Holdings ("INTRACO and UIC steal the limelight", 1986). The UIC bid valued INTRACO at S$127.5 million. At the time, UIC owned 13.4 million INTRACO shares, or 17.9% of its capital and made an offer to acquire a further 61.59 million INTRACO shares that it did not win on the basis of a one-for-one share swap (Cheok, 1986).

However, the proposed takeover of INTRACO by UIC fell through for the following reasons. The UIC bid had come in the midst of a bull market run and the bid of S$1.70 per share was not enough as INTRACO share values had hit a peak of S$2.22 in 1986, that was partly fuelled by the takeover bid itself ("Takeover bids help boost price of three shares", 1986). UIC did not provide evidence that it had the management expertise to get INTRACO's widely diversified assets into good working order ("UIC will have to do better if it hopes to win INTRACO", 1986). In addition, INTRACO's associated companies had helped to shore up its interim performance. For example, INTRACO's 20% interest in the publicly listed Insurance Corporation of Singapore (ICS) enabled the former to receive S$890,600 in profits ("Buoyant associates help shore up INTRACO's earnings", 1986). ICS was 52% owned by DBS Bank, which also owned a 16% interest in INTRACO.

Temasek Holdings had assured INTRACO that it would not divest its 26.7% stake in the company and this boosted the confidence of the company's management team as it restructured the group's trading operations (Cheng, 1986b). Then Temasek deputy chairman, Hwang Peng Yuan, with regard to the speculation on INTRACO, had said that "Temasek [was] not actively seeking a buyer" ("No offer received for INTRACO shares: Temasek", 1988). The board of directors at INTRACO had also recommended that shareholders reject the offer from UIC (McLaughlan, 1986). In 1985, despite difficult trading conditions, INTRACO managed to post a 14.2% increase in group turnover at S$433.27 million from S$379.43 million in 1984 (Jarhom, 1986). However, INTRACO made a fourfold increase in provisions for doubtful debts from S$1.4 million to S$7 million, which resulted in a trading loss for the group at the end of 1985 (Chan, 1986). Nonetheless, having made record provisions for bad debts, INTRACO was well placed to benefit from a recovery in the economy.

Table 5.2 shows INTRACO's financial profile from 1982 to 1986. INTRACO's profit fell to a record low of S$421,000 after tax in 1985 from S$1.9 million in 1984. However, it could be argued that INTRACO's profits were already on a decline in 1982 and 1983, coinciding with the slowdown in the global economy. There was subsequently a rebound of S$6.8 million in 1986 with the improvement in the global economy.

Table 5.2. Five-year Group Financial Profile 1982–1986 ('000).

	1986	**1985**	**1984**	**1983**	**1982**
Turnover	358,706	433,274	379,428	262,060	249,083
Profit before tax	11,166	2,786	4,402	7,066	11,284
Profit after tax	6,890	421	1,964	3,778	6,725
Net current assets	56,816	57,203	57,373	80,241	53,715
Investments	52,234	64,733	69,114	50,859	34,308
Expenditure carried forward	31	160	41	80	38
Fixed assets	50,785	51,681	52,351	27,578	1,473
Minority interests	2,470	4,182	4,810	3,634	3,654
Share capital	75,000	75,000	75,000	75,000	40,000
Reserves	82,580	79,264	81,724	86,168	58,945
Shareholders' equity	157,580	154,264	156,724	161,168	98,945
Per share					
Profit before tax (cents)	14.89	3.71	5.87	11.48	19.82
Profit after tax (cents)	9.19	0.56	2.62	6.14	11.81

Source: INTRACO annual reports.

After it managed to stabilise its operations, in 1987, INTRACO installed a new management team headed by newly appointed managing director Tien Sing Cheong who was recruited from Seagate (Yong, 1990a, b). By 1988, INTRACO had succeeded in rebuilding its image as a well-run international trading company. How was INTRACO able to turn around its performance? After the massive exodus of talent from the group in the mid-1980s, the leaders in the upper echelon implemented a major restructuring exercise in 1986 to streamline business operations (Chandiramani, 1988). These included strengthening management expertise, re-grouping businesses and a critical review and weeding of the company's "lame-duck" subsidiaries and associates (Chandiramani, 1988). INTRACO also appointed three new directors. They were Hwang Peng Yuan and Lam Khin Hui from Temasek Holdings and Ajith Prasad, Director (Budget) from the Ministry of Finance. Hwang Peng Yuan was the Deputy Chairman of Temasek. He had served on the board of several publicly listed companies and was a member of the PSDC that identified INTRACO as one of the GLCs that should be privatised (De Silva, 1987). The new appointments reinforced Temasek's earlier position that it would hold on to its stake in INTRACO for the time being to enable the company to reorganise and consolidate after the recent changes in management (De Silva, 1987).

NEW INDUSTRIES: PETROCHEMICALS

The petrochemicals division was the fastest growing in the 1980s. Its sales figures increased by 32% from 1982 to 1986. The division has two departments: organic chemicals at 23.3% of total group turnover and plastics at 16.4%. Both departments had benefitted from buoyant demand that resulted in rising prices and volume (Chandiramani, 1988). INTRACO also became the sole distributor of the government's share of the chemical by-products from the Petrochemical Complex of Singapore (PCS). PCS accounted for half of INTRACO's entire turnover in chemical products. The other supplies came from complexes in Europe and the Middle East. INTRACO had received fixed margins of 2 to 3% on the sale of petrochemical products (Chandiramani, 1988). The group's main markets were primarily in China, Japan and Taiwan.

In 1982, Singapore refined 500,000 tonnes of crude oil from China and the former was eager to buy more to help replace shipments from Indonesia and Malaysia, which were doing more of their own refining ("Singapore and China: The sweet taste of co-operation", 1989). INTRACO also wanted to swap Chinese naphta for petrochemicals from its new, loss-making S$1 billion plant. China realised that Singapore had an edge over Hong Kong in its wide range of expertise in serving the oil industry, from rig building to oil refining. Moreover, then Mayor of Shenzhen Liang Xiang had commented while on a visit to Singapore in December 1983 that China was keen to learn from Singapore on how to get the best out of Western multinationals ("Singapore and China: The sweet taste of co-operation", 1989).

The divestment process also affected the petrochemicals sector. Oil giant Shell had bought over most of the government's half stake in the S$2 billion petrochemical complex at Pulau Ayer Merbau (Chng, 1989). The complex produced a range of chemical raw materials used to manufacture products like plastics, polyester fibre, synthetic rubber and octane booster for motor gasoline. The Ministry of Finance, Temasek Holdings and DBS Bank were the three Singapore parties involved in the sale. The finance ministry's Permanent Secretary (Revenue) and Chairman of Temasek Holdings, Lee Ek Tieng had commented that the price "represented a satisfactory return on the Government's investments" (Chng, 1989).

INTRACO was the sole distributor for the Singapore government's share of petrochemicals from the government's S$2 billion petrochemical complex. However, the government has sold off its 30% stake in two major petrochemical companies in the complex to Shell Eastern Petroleum, which meant its role was reduced, and INTRACO had to identify new sources of supply for some of their petrochemical products (Lim, 1989a). The Singapore government was also finalising the sale of its entire 50% share in a third company in the complex which housed a total of eight companies. In anticipation of losing some of its petrochemicals trading business, INTRACO had been identifying new sources of supply for some petrochemical products. INTRACO had also looked at ways to offset any fall in petrochemical turnover by raising the business of other divisions (Lim, 1989a).

JOINT VENTURES

INTRACO had managed to increase its foothold in China through a joint venture deal with China Resources in 1985. China Resources Holdings was one of the select groups of corporations backed by the Chinese government in Beijing and empowered to handle trade for mainland China at the time. The company was also the general agency for the various national foreign trade corporations under the Ministry of Foreign Trade Economic Relations in China ("INTRACO explains delay in setting up joint venture with China Resources", 1986). This was INTRACO's first major business expansion move since the management exodus of 1985. The execution of this joint venture was held back by a year because of the management changes and restructuring that took place within the group ("INTRACO explains delay in setting up joint venture with China Resources", 1986). The agreement was signed on 25 November 1985 and with the completion of the reorganisation exercise, the 50–50 joint venture was activated. The joint venture company was called INTRACO Resources.

The much courted China Resources handled the bulk of China's imports and exports through its office in Hong Kong. With the support of INTRACO's international connections, the new company would manage trade between China and other countries using Singapore as a base. In turn, INTRACO Resources could also act as an intermediary for Western companies wanting to trade with China. A potential area that INTRACO wanted to exploit was to take on trade between China and those countries with which Beijing does not have diplomatic relations (Loh, 1986). A portion of such trade was conducted through third parties. Investments in third countries were another opportunity that INTRACO Resources was keen to court. Among the possibilities were timber concessions in Papua New Guinea or oil palm plantations in Malaysia. Sales of the joint venture dealing with timber, textiles and other commodities totalled more than S$100 million in 1989. INTRACO's total turnover was around S$563 million in fiscal year 1988, a 38% increase compared to 1987. However, from 1984 to 1988, INTRACO's return on its equity ranged from 0.3 to 5.2%.

Trade with China contributed about 15% of INTRACO's turnover in 1988. In 1989, after the Tiananmen Square protests in China, INTRACO concluded a second joint-venture agreement with a Chinese state-owned company called China National Packaging Import & Export Corporation (Chinapack) (Siow, 1989). This Chinese foreign trading firm was under the purview of the Chinese Ministry of Foreign Economic Relations and Trade. The joint venture company was named Sintrapack Pte Ltd and was the second INTRACO vehicle dedicated to the China trade. INTRACO would assume a majority stake of 51% in Sintrapack with the balance held by the Chinese company. Sintrapack was mainly involved in trade through Singapore to China in packaging materials such as paper and pulp, metals, plastics, plywood and rubber. The joint venture company would also engage in the sales of China-made packaging products overseas and sales of packaging equipment and machinery in China. At a later date, it would offer consultancy services to the packaging and food processing industries.

The third joint venture between China's state-owned companies and INTRACO was Sintra Merchants. This joint venture supplied fuel and raw materials like liquefied gas, petroleum, bulk chemicals and fertilisers to the Shekou industrial zone. It also traded in steel, minerals and plywood for export to China and re-exported processed goods from the Shekou industrial zone (Yong, 1990a, b). INTRACO's management was convinced that the partnerships with socialist economies would provide the group with a more stable and lucrative source of income instead of merely playing the middle role of buying and selling of goods.

GROWTH AREAS

The company added 25 new staff in 1989. New managing director Tien said that, "the training of staff, upgrading of staff and adding people with new skills certainly will be an on-going exercise" (Lim, 1989a). He was of the view that INTRACO must cope with changes in the petrochemicals business, which was one of the company's fastest growing divisions (Lim, 1989b). INTRACO attributed its record turnover in 1988 to the excellent trading conditions especially in the markets for petroleum chemicals and plastics.

Perception was another key area of concern for INTRACO. There was a misperception that INTRACO was still a government trading company. Tien had said that, "the perception has worked in our favour as we work outside Singapore … but it gives the wrong impression in the eyes of the public who think we're favoured, that we have special privileges. There's no such thing today. We're really out there competing for business like any other company. That's something that we hope we can change in the minds of Singaporeans" (Lim, 1989b).

Another concern for Tien was INTRACO's lack of presence in the business and investment community. He said, "Every night, I look at the volume of stocks traded on television but I never see INTRACO. It's never been picked up on the list of most active stocks. I would like to see more interest in INTRACO stock" (Lim, 1989b). According to Margaret Woo, an investment analyst at Phillips Securities, INTRACO had not been able to leave behind its image of being a government-backed company. The analyst described INTRACO as "a good company [that] is underperforming all the time". She added that investors neglect INTRACO because it was not in the "in" industries such as marine, property and hotels (Lim, 1989b).

According to Tien, as INTRACO headed into a new decade, to improve the company's standing, "our task is really to ensure that INTRACO can provide a useful service in everything we do, our customers and suppliers believe we're providing a useful service and profits we make commensurate with the type of service we're providing" (Lim, 1989b). Tien explained, "This is a people game — to find the right people to do it. I think the skills of a chief executive officer are to be able not only to identify the right people to help you make the thing happen" (Lim, 1989b). This emphasises the importance of leadership in shaping the fast evolving trading industry.

EXTERNAL SHOCKS

The Chinese government's crackdown on pro-democracy protesters at Tiananmen Square in 1989 was expected to impact bilateral economic relations. INTRACO Limited was the second company to announce a new joint venture project with China in the post-crackdown era (Oh, 1989). The first was Inno-pac that was involved in setting up chicken farms and Shakey's Pizza parlour.

Figure 5.1 shows the turnover against profit from 1980 to 2003. As this chapter examines the period from 1980 to 1990, the graph shows that the

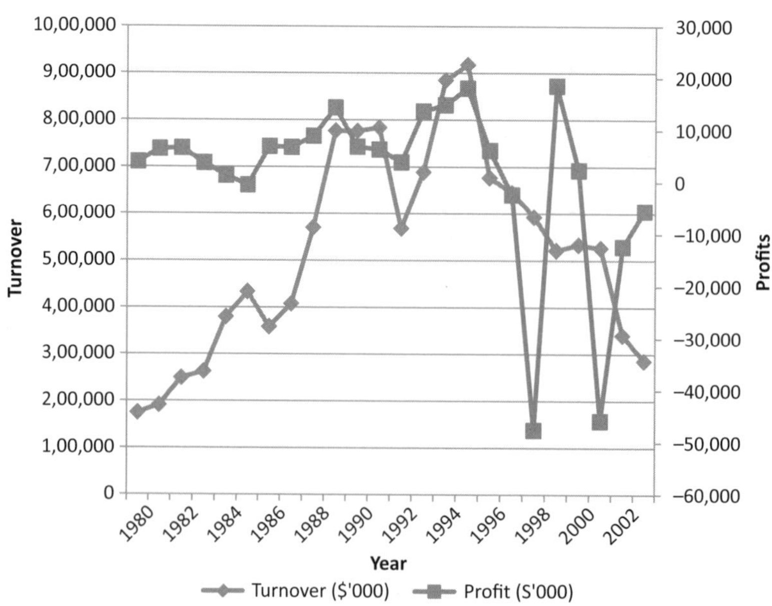

Figure 5.1. Turnover Against Profit (1980–2003).

turnover for INTRACO was generally on a positive upward trend from 1980 to 1990. In 1980, the turnover was valued at S$175 million, rising to S$790 million in 1990. This trend of rising turnover suffered a downturn in 1986 when INTRACO underwent the exodus of its senior management and the company became a takeover target from UIC. After Temasek shored up INTRACO with the secondment of two senior DBS executives and refused to sell its stake in the company to UIC, and with the recruitment of new senior executives, the turnover continued to rise until 1990. The trend for profits showed that the company started from approximately S$2 million in 1980 and rose to a high of S$12 million in 1989 before decreasing to S$8 million in 1990. Earnings per share were significantly higher in the earlier years, as the shares issued could have been smaller with a larger profit amount being shared by smaller group of investors.

Profits were on the positive side from 1980 to 1995 with a slight upslope indicating slight increases in profits. There were minor dips in 1986 and 1992, but profits were still positive and high because turnover for INTRACO was robust. There were minor losses during 1986 turnover dip but in 1992, a dip in turnover still returned profits, which could be due to lower level of expenses. Between 1996 and 2003, the company experienced yearly decrease in turnover. Profits after 1996 were volatile, and often fell on the negative side.

Chapter 6 examines the twilight years of INTRACO as a GLC and its eventual takeover by a foreign corporation PSC based in Hong Kong. The writer was informed that a bid from a consortium of former INTRACO executives was rejected in favour of the bid from PSC (Interviews with former INTRACO senior executives on 7 July 2011 and 12 July 2011). It was unfortunate that the "Ex-INTRACO" bid was not successful because the consortium had wanted to revamp INTRACO and transform the company into a successful trading outfit once again. The former INTRACO executives knew the strengths and weaknesses of the company and could have possibly turned around the company's fortunes.

CHAPTER 6

POST-COLD WAR AND GLOBALISATION — 1990 TO 2000

POST-COLD WAR ENVIRONMENT

Entering a new decade in 1990, analysts generally felt that INTRACO was well positioned to take advantage of major global events that had been shaping the international economy since the end of the Cold War. Perestroika in the Soviet Union and the expansion of economic reforms were transforming Eastern Europe and Vietnam and brought both challenges and opportunities to INTRACO (Yong, 1990a). The new millennium also triggered a wave of mergers and acquisitions among companies. Domestically, in June 2000, the Monetary Authority of Singapore (MAS) announced a three-year deadline for local banks to dispose of their non-core assets and for government-linked companies (GLCs) to follow suit. This announcement became part of the growing debate on the role of GLCs in Singapore. Then, GLCs were accused of "crowding out" competition from the local small and medium enterprises (SMEs) and of neglecting their primary role of venturing overseas to create an external economic wing for Singapore. Critics had pointed out that the stock exchange was dominated by GLCs and this had to change if more listings from foreign companies were to be realised.

In the midst of these developments, INTRACO regrouped its diverse businesses into three sectors: hydrocarbon resources, industrial goods and electronics (Yong, 1990b). The hydrocarbon resources group included petroleum, petrochemicals, plastics, textiles, paper and food. The industrial group consisted of building materials, engineering products, electrical products, metals and minerals. One of the key concerns was that profit margins were extremely thin, highlighting the group's need to move beyond purely being a broker or middleman role. The profit margin in 1989 was 1.3%, but in 1990, it slipped further to 0.9%.

In 1990, the Chief Executive Officer (CEO) of INTRACO Tien Sing Cheong was appointed a director and Managing Director of INTRACO. He joined INTRACO in October 1988 as the Chief Operating Officer and became the CEO in March 1989. With a new management team in place and problematic areas such as inventory and foreign exchange controls rectified — such as the S$6.5 million write-off in the value of inventory in plastics in 1988 — the company seemed to have left its troubles behind (Yong, 1990b). Tien made several management changes to ensure that more senior executives were involved in INTRACO's core businesses and identified with the company's strategic directions. He had also taken on the post of deputy general manager in charge of INTRACO's food and electronics portfolios. INTRACO's deputy general manager for corporate planning and business development Sam Chong Keen was responsible for timber; investments came under the purview of Charles Phan, a deputy general manager; while general manager Thang Kwek Min focused more on countertrade, or barter trade (Lim, 1989).

According to Tien, it would be difficult for INTRACO to grow if it remained in a middleman role for a 5% mark-up ceiling, because there would be many competitors offering a mark up of 1% less. He said, "we must be able to add value and useful service" (Lim, 1989). At the time, INTRACO had some S$75 million in addition to the earlier $36 million as surplus funds, considered to be a sizeable financial war chest for a Singapore company. Tien said that, "we see ourselves identifying more upstream, downstream vertical integration opportunities" (Lim, 1989). Although it would be harder to find 5 to 10 strong executives to manage smaller projects instead of a few strong executives to manage a large project, Tien preferred to place his bets on several smaller projects. His goal was to "go for possible higher return and cover bases than to put all $25 million in one project". He also added that the skills for a CEO included the ability to identify the right project and people to make deals happen (Lim, 1989).

In discussing the poor performance of INTRACO in the past, Tien said, "looking back, I think some of the mistakes were due to the fact that we went into businesses that we knew very little about, or where we had only a small role to play" ("INTRACO set for a brisk revival", 1990). Like a number of other GLCs, INTRACO also set up its own treasury division to invest its growing cash surpluses and better manage its foreign exchange risks. The treasury division was one of two new service divisions set up by INTRACO in 1989 to enhance support for its trading division and to strengthen its management control (Balan, 1990). The other new divisions were the internal control and audit division to monitor commercial practices and operations. The new divisions were created partly in response to the disastrous write-offs from 1988 to 1989 when profits were adversely affected by the collapse in plastic prices and the plywood scam (Balan, 1990). INTRACO managed to build up a healthy cash flow and reserves in 1989. INTRACO chairman P.Y. Hwang said: "This trend provides the impetus for our plan to move into value-added activities through integration and diversification" (Balan, 1990).

Tien explained this: "We ask ourselves what up and downstream that we can do. I think these are all the questions we've to ask ourselves and sensibly evaluate all those opportunities" (Lim, 1989). Sam Chong Keen, INTRACO's deputy general manager, explained that this rationalisation process of moving into upstream activities would include joint ventures in manufacturing and the acquisition of yarn factories and timber mills in countries such as Indonesia, Malaysia, Myanmar and Thailand (Tan, 1989). The aim was to provide INTRACO with better control over the supply of products for its middleman role. Sam commented, "It's like having our own brand name. You can also control the pricing, customer service and even quality" (Tan, 1989). This strategy would mean greater investments, but the returns would also be higher. For example, a timber mill's earnings' margin is some 15 to 20%, while the middleman receives between 4 and 6% or less. Another benefit would be the ability to monitor and ensure that the quality of the sawn timber is consistent (Tan, 1989). Tien remarked then that "we can either invest in a mill or work with European distributors that maintain warehouses in Europe to tie-up either end so that there's no danger of buyers short-circuiting you. The business now requires traders to be more committed, more integrated, to move up

Table 6.1. Key Investments of INTRACO.

Companies	Share %	Products	Announcement date
Samara Motors (S) Pte Ltd	51	Cars	January 1989
LM Food Industries Pte Ltd	20	Frozen meat	January 1989
Sintrapack Pte Ltd	51	Packaging products	July 1989
Hexa Timber (S) Pte Ltd	70	Timber & wood related products	November 1989
Burwill Holdings Ltd	21	Metals	December 1989
Russalmaz Asia Pte Ltd	25	Diamond	December 1989
IntElorg	31	Electronics	January 1990

Source: "INTRACO set for a brisk revival", *Asian Finance*, July 1990.

and down the spectrum" (Lim, 1989). Table 6.1 shows the main business subsidiaries under INTRACO in the late 1980s.

INTRACO's improved performance at the start of the 1990s can be attributed to its "house cleaning" exercise undertaken in 1989. Several business lines that were marginally profitable or unrelated to the company's overall thrust were sold. For example, the company sold its cigarette distribution agency back to its principal because they had no role to play. Instead, INTRACO had focused on its strengths and expanded into activities where synergy within the group could be achieved ("INTRACO set for a brisk revival", 1990). For example, the company acquired a 21% stake in Hong Kong listed metals trader Burwill International for HK$71.2 million. Tien commented at the time that "the acquisition not only gave us an important foothold in the domestic market, but I think we can do a few more things from now on" ("INTRACO set for a brisk revival", 1990). The link with Burwill enabled INTRACO to tap into the former's commodity trading network in China, Hong Kong, Southeast Asia, Australia and the Eastern Bloc (Yong, 1990b).

Tien was of the view that "just because we are government-controlled doesn't mean that we have to be pigeon-holed as such. Look at what Singapore Airlines has achieved, though it is in the same position" ("INTRACO set for a brisk revival", 1990). Countertrade is another area where INTRACO could expand its activities. Tien's take on countertrade was that "it's not just a standalone function, but will complement the activities of the other divisions, particularly in the areas of trade relating to socialist countries" (Lim, 1989). Exchanging goods for other goods was one way of dealing with the problem of non-freely convertible currencies from the socialist countries.

For example, to effectively penetrate the Russian market, INTRACO struck a deal with IntElorg, a Soviet central purchasing agency. Through IntElorg, INTRACO sourced Russian timber, mineral ores and petrochemical products for export to other parts of the world. These products were passed to INTRACO and then sold for hard currency to finance the export of consumer electronic products to Russia through the joint venture company (Mulchand, 1990). IntElorg was seen by INTRACO as a model of strategic alliance with giant business partners. In 1989, IntElorg recorded sales of S$4 billion. As a central buying agency, IntElorg imported personal computers and electronic products for Soviet customers. Many of its clients were large industrial organisations that produced commodities for export (Yong, 1990a). Tien believed that a "screwdriver" strategy, which is little more than a simple assembly job that involves a relatively small capital outlay, could work between INTRACO and Russia. He said, "we can turn hardware over to the Soviets and let them figure their own software" (Mulchand, 1990). Vladamir Vershinin, deputy trade representative at the Soviet embassy in Singapore commented that the joint venture also represented, in part, Russia's plans to look increasingly towards Asia.

In 1990, INTRACO also explored the possibility of assembling its own computers for export to Russia. INTRACO had to establish a brand of computers before deciding if it will control production by manufacturing the personal computers on its own. However, Tien explained that even if the company assembled its own computers, it would still have to buy a lot of sub-assemblies from the region. INTRACO did not push into the computer assembly line but created an information technology (IT) department to develop software programmes for client firms (Yong, 1990a, November).

One of the key risks in the former Soviet Union was political uncertainty, such as the Lithuanian separatist movement at the time. Sam Chong Keen acknowledged at the time that "these things are on our minds ... but what are the alternatives? Do we wait? We have a business to run and business is about dealing with uncertainty" (Kwang, 1990). INTRACO had also formed a joint venture with the Soviet Union's sole diamond producer and exporter, Almaz. INTRACO owned a 25% share in its new company, Russalmaz Asia. The company aimed to be a "sighting centre" for wholesalers from Australia to Japan.

Within the region, INTRACO stepped up its counter trade operations. The company signed several bilateral agreements. Deals have also been concluded with the communist regimes of China, Cambodia and Vietnam in plastic raw materials, bitumen, timber, sugar, palm oil and other food products (Balan, 1990). In Vietnam, INTRACO had a representative office in Ho Chi Minh City and another in Hanoi ("INTRACO and Informatics in Vietnam venture", 1994).

In line with its business expansion, INTRACO also invested about S$2.5 million to upgrade its computer systems in 1990. The aim was to integrate all the subsidiaries and divisions of the company ("INTRACO invests S$2.5 m to revamp computer system", 1990). The upgrade in computerisation was administered by local company Engineering Computer Services (ECS) and among the specialised applications were financial investment, cash management packages, project management and personnel systems. ECS was founded in 1982 and its shareholders included Natsteel (48%) and Hewlett Packard (9%). ECS comprised five divisions specialising in healthcare, engineering, manufacturing, services and micro-computers ("INTRACO invests S$2.5 m to revamp computer system", 1990). The manager of the ECS Financial Services Division Alan Wee had said, "Time and information are critical in a trading company. With the new computerised system, the sales and purchasing system is linked to accounting and inventory, and managers can check on stocks available or credit status at any time" ("INTRACO invests S$2.5 m to revamp computer system", 1990).

CONFLICTS AND CRISES IN THE DECADE

The invasion of Kuwait by Iraq triggered the Gulf War of 1990 that rattled many companies including INTRACO but also presented opportunities for Sintra Oil, a wholly-owned subsidiary in the oil trading business.

INTRACO's exposure to the oil crisis was minimal because it did not carry oil-related products in its inventory.

The Yugoslav Wars (Bosnia War) from 1992 to 1995 also affected Singapore companies such as INTRACO because of the United Nations economic embargo on the Yugoslavian states of Serbia and Montenegro (Phua, 1992). INTRACO's general manager Michael Lee had assured that the company traded mainly in consumer electronics products with Slovenia but not in large quantities.

The Asian Financial Crisis in 1998 had an impact on INTRACO in terms of divestment of government shares in GLCs and restructuring of their non-core assets. Estimated total value on non-core assets ranged from S$3 million to over S$6 million, but the pace of divestment was gradual and not aggressive (Wong, 1999). The crisis did cause problems for INTRACO, and one of the regional countries that it had to pull out of was Indonesia (Kagda, 2003).

GAINING A FOOTHOLD IN THE FOOD INDUSTRIES

In June 1989, INTRACO took an initial 25% stake and later raised it to 40% in Leong Moh, a distributor in fresh and frozen meat to form a new company called LM Food Industries with a paid up capital of S$2 million (Yong, 1990a). INTRACO wanted to expand its share of the local fresh and frozen meat market by investing in the company (Chia, 1989). An INTRACO spokesperson had said, "Leong Moh has been distributing INTRACO's frozen meat products for many years and this acquisition is both a logical and strategic step for INTRACO to secure its distribution network and increase its share in the frozen meat business" (Chia, 1989).

Leong Moh had acquired Singapore Animal Husbandry Enterprises in 1988 for about S$1 million after the cash-strapped mini-mart chain was placed under judicial management to protect it from its creditors (Chia, 1989). With the acquisition, Leong Moh had a modern semi-automated air-conditioned deboning facility and chiller room that could accommodate up to 400 pigs' carcasses. With the new partnership, Leong Moh could tap into INTRACO's resources and supply contacts. It also formalised the business relationship that already existed between the two companies. LM

Food Industries was tasked to build cold rooms and embarked on the processing of specialty meat items.

Venturing into the region, in early 1996, INTRACO had formed a consortium with Hiap Huat, Thakral and CWT Distribution Ltd through its subsidiary Camsin Corporation to team up with the Cambodian provincial government of Takeo to grow rice. The Singapore consortium would lease a 10,000-hectare site in the province. A spokesperson for the group had commented that the Singaporean consortium would assist the Cambodian government to grow two to three rice crops a year. The consortium would build an irrigation system, automate agriculture and export the rice. The consortium would also form two joint venture companies in Cambodia. The first joint-venture company, Takeo Farmers' Trust Ltd, was incorporated in Cambodia with the Cambodian government taking a majority 60% stake. The other 40% stake was equally divided among the four Singaporean companies ("Consortium of S'pore firms enters ventures with Cambodia", 1996). The other joint-venture company, Consortium Marketing (S) Pte Ltd, had an authorised capital of S$200,000 and a paid-up capital of S$100,000, and would manage the export and marketing of rice and other agricultural products. INTRACO would take a 10% stake in the company, while Camsin, Hiap Huat and Thakral would each hold a 15% share ("Consortium of S'pore firms enters ventures with Cambodia", 1996). The Cambodian government would take up the remaining stake.

FISHERIES

In 1994, INTRACO formed a joint venture with its Russian partners in the port city of Vladivostok to source and process seafood products for export. Its Russian partner was Intraros, comprising entrepreneurs who provided the technical expertise in fishing operations ("INTRACO forms seafood processing venture in Russian Far East", 1994). Intraros had an authorised capital of S$80,000 and a paid-up capital of S$68,000. INTRACO had 70% share of the joint venture and Russian individuals held the rest. Intraros would complement the activities of INTRACO Foods. Food was one of INTRACO's four core businesses. INTRACO Foods' product range extended from seafood, meat and poultry to fruit, canned foods and dairy products. INTRACO CEO Bernard Chen had said of the joint venture at the time: "our aim is to focus on the development and expansion of core business of food and food processing. The Russian Far East region was rich in seafood and marine products such as Pollack, cod, salmon, herring, scallops and crabs which have a ready market in China, Europe, Japan and the US". Chen had said that "our aim is to focus on the development and expansion of our core business of food and food processing, particularly higher value-added activities such as Intraros' fishing and on board processing" ("INTRACO forms seafood processing venture in Russian Far East", 1994). He added, "We intend to expand our fleet of fishing vessels in the future to ensure a strong supply of seafood products which we will distribute to our established markets in Japan, Europe and the US".

BROKERING FOR EASTERN EUROPE

INTRACO's trading business was adversely affected by difficult market conditions and the political uncertainties in Eastern Europe in the early 1990s when it encountered soft commodity prices and a fall in demand. As part of its expansion into the food industry and the Russian Far East market, in August 1993, INTRACO shipped 2,500 tonnes of chicken worth more than US$2 million from the United States to Vladivostok. Reportedly, other third-country business deals involving Russia that INTRACO helped to conclude were the purchase of frozen seafood in bulk for export to Europe and the United States as well as supplying Russia with meat, dairy goods, seafood, wool, fruit, grain and other produce from Western Australia ("INTRACO expands food trading business in Russia", 1993).

CHANGE IN MANAGEMENT PERSONNEL

In early 1990, INTRACO general manager for countertrade Thang Kwek Min resigned to join Representations International Pte Ltd, a local private company aiming to expand its regional business. Representations International was formed in 1972 by the late Ted De Ponti and started out as a manufacturers' representative in the tobacco industry in Singapore, Malaysia and Indonesia. Since then it had expanded into fertiliser and industrial chemicals and branched out into the Philippines and China

("INTRACO GM to join local private company", 1990). Thang joined Representations International as group general manager and managing director designate. He would be responsible for developing the company's international trading business in agriculture and other products including countertrade.

When Thang joined INTRACO in 1969, he was instrumental in developing trade links with China as well as INTRACO's countertrade business. However, his duties as general manager had been substantially taken over by managing director Tien and deputy general manager for corporate planning and investments Sam Chong Keen. Nonetheless, Thang agreed to serve on the board of some of the companies in the INTRACO group which had active dealings with China ("INTRACO GM to join local private company", 1990).

A few years later, in early 1994, Sam Chong Keen also resigned to become the managing director of NTUC Comfort Holdings ("Keeping cool and comfortable in the driver's seat", 1994). Upon joining INTRACO in 1987, he had said: "I felt then that Singapore was such a small place that, to be worth your salt, you needed to go overseas. I systematically scouted for opportunities amongst large public-listed companies and INTRACO fitted the bill because it was then one of the few companies that was truly international and has business dealings with almost 40 countries" ("Keeping cool and comfortable in the driver's seat", 1990). The loss of senior management for INTRACO was reminiscent of what had occurred in the mid-1980s and called for a re-evaluation of INTRACO's business focus. The recruitment of senior staff to replace those that had left was critical as it determined the future of the company in a post-Cold War environment.

ADOPTING SPECIFIC COUNTRY APPROACHES

In the early 1990s, INTRACO had embarked on a country approach in its trading activities to focus on countries in which the group has particular strengths ("INTRACO's new country approach", 1992). CEO Bernard Chen had explained that part of this new approach would be the establishment of regional representative offices. More of this strategy emerged at INTRACO's 25th anniversary dinner in November 1993 where

INTRACO Chairman Hwang Peng Yuan had disclosed that the company would also establish business bases in Cambodia and Myanmar and India and Pakistan. He had added, "Ultimately, we hope to trade not only between these countries and Singapore, but among them as well" ("INTRACO to widen base of businesses", 1993).

Hwang had said before, "We will continue to focus on our core businesses and strengthen our existing base" ("INTRACO's new country approach", 1992). However, he had also noted that, "we are acutely aware that simple trading no longer meets the needs of our customers. We must instead provide services that will attract new customers and encourage existing ones to increase their business with us" ("INTRACO to widen base of businesses", 1993). To achieve better synergy within the company, the electronics and electrical divisions were also merged.

ENHANCING ITS POSITION IN THE OIL BUSINESS

INTRACO also consolidated its petroleum business under wholly-owned subsidiary Sintra Oil Pte Ltd that was involved in the physical trading of bunker oil and had taken over the oil trading activities that were directly handled by INTRACO (Hadhi, 1990). Sintra Oil was established in 1983 as a joint venture between INTRACO and SNOC Pte Ltd. INTRACO bought the remaining shares from SNOC to use Sintra as a vehicle to diversify into the bunker oil and petroleum business (Hadhi, 1990). INTRACO established a joint venture company called Sintra Merchants Pte Ltd with the China Merchants group of Hong Kong in 1990 to supply petroleum and chemical products for distribution throughout southern China and assist INTRACO in expanding its activities in China and other parts of Asia ("INTRACO set to expand role as oil trader", 1990). INTRACO's managing director Tien would be the company's chairman while its operations would be overseen by INTRACO's deputy general manager (hydrocarbon resources) Seah Chong Leng, who would be the managing director of Sintra Merchants Pte Ltd ("INTRACO–HK joint venture to supply fuel to S. China", 1990).

The joint venture was part of INTRACO's strategy of forging alliances with strong trading partners to penetrate more markets. INTRACO held a 51% share of Sintra Merchants. The remaining stake was held equally by subsidiaries China Merchants Development Co Ltd and CMSNC Shekou Industrial Area Petrochemical Corporation ("INTRACO set to expand role as oil trader", 1990). China Merchants was a diversified group with more than 300 companies in China and Hong Kong. At the time, they were involved in shipping, shipbuilding, tourism, construction, banking and manufacturing (Koh, 1990). One of its projects was the development of the Shekou Industrial Zone into a port town. Shekou, located in Shenzhen, serves as the distribution point to other special economic zones in southern China. China Merchants Holdings was an investment arm of China's Ministry of Communications and made history when it took on the task of developing Shekou from a desolate fishing village into an industrial port. As it is strategically located in southern China, facing the South China Sea, Shekou was considered the best logistics base for oil exploration activities ("China Merchants in yet another joint venture", 1990).

Shekou was part of the fast-growing Shenzhen special economic zone, where demand for oil refineries in the region was expected to be strong. China Merchants was also keen to gain a foothold in Southeast Asia to meet its long-term requirements (Koh, 1990). Sintra Merchants had delivered a gas and oil shipment of more than US$800,000 to Shekou in 1990. The company had signed a six-month contract with a Singapore refinery to supply 8,000 metric tonnes of liquefied petroleum gas to the industrial zone.

INTRACO recruited a professional oil trader Johan Berman and appointed him as general manager in the petrochemical department to enhance the company's position in oil and related products. Berman was formerly with leading international oil and commodities trader Marc Rich and Co. and was its trading manager in Singapore. He had 13 years of experience in commodities trading in Europe, United States and Asia (Hadhi, 1990). INTRACO released a statement saying that the development would "enhance its international trading position for products such as petrochemicals, plastics and textiles as well as for other subsidiaries in oil and oil-related products" (Hadhi, 1990). This consolidated move would also strengthen INTRACO's capabilities in transacting counter trade deals with refineries and petrochemical complexes such as those in China.

A SLICE OF THE REGION'S INFRASTRUCTURAL DEVELOPMENT

In the early 1990s, the government began to encourage Singapore companies to form consortiums to expand into the region. Senior Minister of State for Trade and Industry Lim Boon Heng suggested that through a "Singapore Inc" approach, Singapore-based MNCs, GLCs and other large local companies could lead the way, supported by smaller home-grown supporting firms (Teh, 1992). Following this, INTRACO, Sembawang Engineering and the Public Utilities Board's fully-owned consultancy arm, Development Resources, signed a memorandum of understanding to jointly bid for power plant and power distribution projects in the region (Teh, 1992). No new company would be established as the combination of the consortium needed to first be tested to evaluate how successful it would be. Initially, China, Vietnam and the Philippines would become the consortium's main markets because these economies were starting to open up and Singapore companies were more likely to succeed due to cultural compatibility (Teh, 1992).

Singapore and Vietnam signed a trade agreement in September 1992 while earlier in the year, both countries had also signed a shipping and bilateral air services agreement. Vietnam's reconstruction programme was expected to generate demand for infrastructure construction and engineering services ("More companies set to move into Vietnam with new trade pact", 1992). The Singapore consortium was awarded a major contract to build a S$80 million power generation plant in Vietnam. The consortium's power plant came under the jurisdiction of the Vietnamese state-run Power Company No. 2, which was responsible for the generation and supply of electricity to 16 southern provinces and cities that had a population of 24 million (Mehta, 1993). The consortium would supply power from the 50- to 60-megawatt diesel engine-driven power plant in south Vietnam to state-run power firms that would in turn sell the power to their customers (Mehta, 1993). The consortium shared responsibilities in the following manner: Development Resources conducted feasibility studies and engineering design; INTRACO supplied power generation, transmission and distribution equipment; and Sembawang Corporation was tasked with detailed engineering, construction and installation.

INTRACO chose infrastructure as part of its core area of business under the purview of its technical products and services division and tendered for a number of major infrastructure projects (Cua, 1995). In 1995, INTRACO joined a consortium led by France's Matra Transport to tender for contracts in Singapore's first Light Rail Transit (LRT) system (Divyanathan, 1995).

A NEW INDUSTRY — INFORMATION AND COMMUNICATIONS TECHNOLOGY

INTRACO also ventured into new knowledge-based industries such as information and communications technology (ICT). In late 1994, INTRACO formed a joint venture with Informatics Holdings to establish computer training centres in Vietnam. INTRACO had a 70% stake while Informatics held a 30% stake in INTRACO-Informatics, which was based in Singapore ("INTRACO and Informatics in Vietnam venture", 1994). The joint venture had an authorised capital of S$3 million and a paid-up capital of S$600,000. The first training centre was built in Ho Chi Minh City. INTRACO CEO Bernard Chen said: "We hope to capitalise on this partnership to gain direct access to the masses for the marketing and distribution of computers, computer peripherals and other IT software to complement our electronic business" ("INTRACO and Informatics in Vietnam venture", 1994).

In 1994, INTRACO also bought a 34.3% stake in a local telecommunications company, Teledata (Singapore) Pte Ltd. A spokesman for INTRACO had said that the "the acquisition represents a strategic long-term investment for INTRACO in the telecommunications" ("INTRACO buys Teledata stake", 1994). Teledata consisted of principals from the US, Japan and Europe and distributed 40 different brands of data and voice communications projects such as PABX telephones, electronic phone banking systems, modems and multiplexers (Ng, 1994). Its clientele included Singapore Telecom, banks and multinationals. The Electronic Road Pricing (ERP) was one of its projects (Ng, 1994). Its strategic partnership with main board-listed INTRACO would provide synergy for the two to further explore supplier networks in Eastern Europe, China, Vietnam and Russia. Teledata had planned to tap INTRACO's overseas links (Ng, 1994). With the acquisition, INTRACO in turn aimed to expand

and complement the existing activities undertaken by its electronics division to become a major regional player in the field of data and voice communications ("INTRACO buys Teledata stake", 1994). In 1996, Teledata became a subsidiary of INTRACO when the latter increased its stake in the telecoms firm from 27.4 to 50.8% (Raj, 1998a).

In 1998, Teledata led a consortium called P2P Communications Ltd consisting of itself, NatSteel and US firm, General Telephone and Electronics (GTE), based in Connecticut. The consortium was awarded Singapore's third mobile phone license costing some S$600 million after Singapore Telecom and Mobile One (Raj, 1998a). Subsequently, the Telecommunications Authority of Singapore (TAS) withdrew the cellular phone license after GTE Corp denied it was part of the consortium. P2P explained that General Telephone and Electronics (GTE), was approached to join the consortium after another prospective foreign partner had withdrawn from it before the tender closed on 31 December 1997. Therefore, there was insufficient time to complete any joint venture agreement, but the tendering procedures allowed for the consortium to be incorporated after the award of the tender. The US telecommunications giant GTE explained that while it had an option to take up a 30% stake in P2P in December 1997, it informed P2P in January 1998 that it was unlikely to do so.

As a result of this, the TAS had to revise its tender submission process to require all tendering consortiums to include their joint agreements when they submit their bids. An investigation by the Standing Committee in the Ministry of Finance led Teledata (Singapore) Ltd to be banned from all government contracts for two years from 6 October 1998. INTRACO's chairman and CEO Bernard Chen, in a letter to shareholders, explained that, "we have been advised and are satisfied that the Teledata management had acted in complete good faith throughout. Nevertheless, the TAS inquiry report which had been accepted by the SCOD (Finance Ministry's Standing Committee on Debarment) had found Teledata responsible for negligent misrepresentation" (Raj, 1998b). Chen added, "In this unfortunate episode, Teledata had always been transparent in its approach and in fact had been extremely co-operative in providing the authorities with all the necessary information and documents". Chen added that Teledata had taken steps to "ameliorate the effects of this disbarment" and was appealing against the disbarment (Raj, 1998b). While the disbarment did not prevent Teledata from servicing existing public sector contracts that it had secured earlier, SCOD has advised the ministries and departments concerned to exercise close supervision over the execution of these contracts until they expired. It was not known how much Teledata depended on the government for its business. In March 1999, the deputy chairman of Teledata (Singapore) Ltd Tay Kim Hock resigned (Teh, 1999). He was also INTRACO's chief operating officer and point man for the group's thrust into the telecommunications field (Teh, 1999).

THE ASIAN FINANCIAL CRISIS AND GRADUAL DIVESTMENT OF GLCS

The Asian Financial Crisis was partly the impetus for Singapore companies to focus on their core businesses towards the end of the 1990s. GLCs were expected to take the lead in restructuring their non-core assets. In an interview in mid-1999, Edwin Tay, the research head at BT Brokerage and Associates said, "the GLC restructuring are definitely coming in because many have drifted and diversified too far away from their core businesses" (Wong, 1999). He added that the GLCs "are restructuring partly in response to the crisis and partly because of what is happening globally" (Wong, 1999).

Figure 6.1 shows the trend of turnover rate for INTRACO against profit from 1980 to 2002. The turnover rate dropped from S$790 million in 1990 to S$580 million in 1992 after the end of the Cold War. Singapore had established diplomatic relations with China in 1990, which meant that local companies could trade freely with China without having to pay and provide information for the CESS tax. In short, INTRACO lost its role as a middleman or conduit for local business with China.

INTRACO also had a change of CEO when Bernard Chen took over the company from Tien Sing Cheong in 1990. Profit declined to S$200,000 in 1992 but steadily increased to S$1.8 million in 1996. The turnover rose to above S$900 million in 1996 on the back of strong trading with Eastern European countries, especially Russia, but began to decrease in the middle of the decade and reached a low of S$510 million between 1999 and 2000. After the Asian Financial Crisis, the profit plunged to a loss of S$4.8 million in 1998.

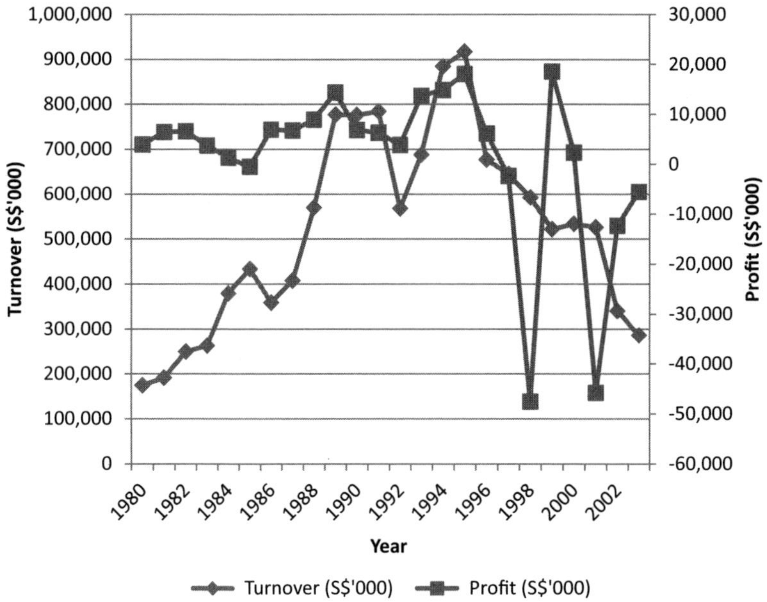

Figure 6.1. INTRACO's Turnover Against Profit (1980–2002).

Figure 6.2 shows the relationship between the turnover generated in Singapore and outside Singapore and shows that there was very little shape relation, maybe only in the early 1990s. Profit then increased dramatically in 1999 to reach S$1.8 million before plunging to a loss of S$4.5 million in 2000.

The significant increase of revenue in the late 1990s to early 2000s generated outside of Singapore seemed to have very little impact on overall turnover, suggesting that most of its profits came from business interests within Singapore. This indicated that the Asian Financial Crisis and terms of currency depreciation of regional economies had significant impact on the turnover of INTRACO. During the crisis, ASEAN countries that sold primary products and commodities took a beating while manufacturing sectors of these countries also suffered because they could not cover their cost overseas. The depreciation in regional currencies meant that INTRACO as a trading company was able to increase its profit margins through the relatively stable Singapore currency to gain greater external

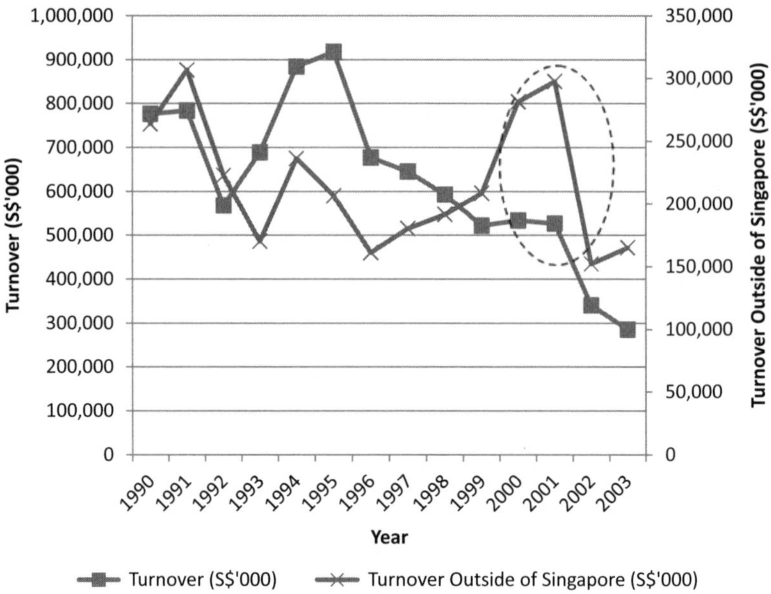

Figure 6.2. Turnover Rate of INTRACO Against Overseas Singapore Profits (1990–2003).

turnover by trading with non-affected countries overseas. However, this effect would not last more than a year or two and ceased in 2000.

Figure 6.3 shows that both internal and external revenue suffered because of the 1991 Gulf War, which adversely affected business globally. The downward trend reversed after 1993, both internally and externally. INTRACO's turnover in Singapore reached a peak of more than S$700 million in 1995, which was three times more than external turnover of S$250 million. It seemed that INTRACO was not able to make significant business impact overseas and was mainly reliant on its domestic business interests for revenue.

From 1980 to 2003, which included the period of the Cold War, its demise and increasing global economic integration, INTRACO was not able to enhance its business and trade linkages overseas and its profit margin continued to decline.

In May 2001, Au Eng Fong was appointed as one of the directors and the CEO of INTRACO. He was formerly heading his own group of trading

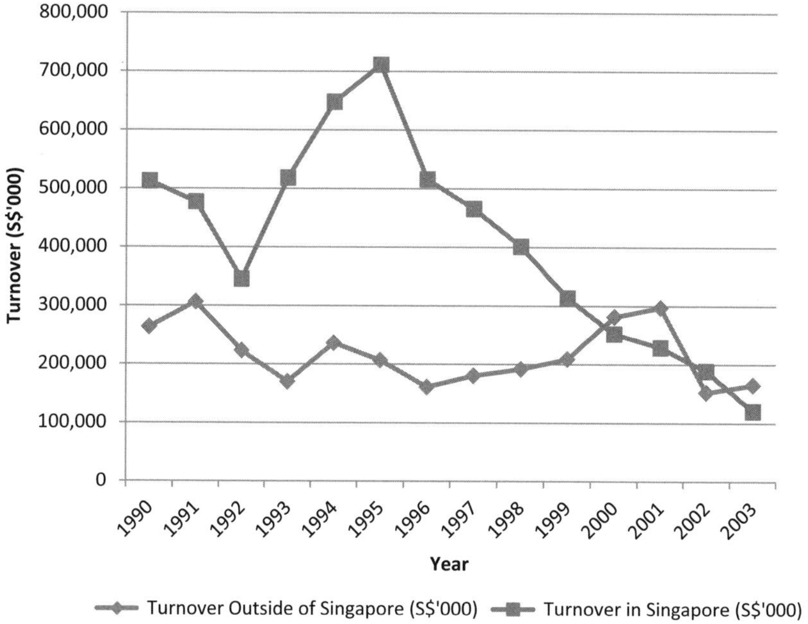

Figure 6.3. Share of Revenue for INTRACO Within Singapore versus Outside of Singapore (1990–2003).

companies. His key task was to streamline and rationalise the group's businesses (Lee, 2001). He left by the end of 2001 after completing his tasks at INTRACO. A cash payout of some S$50.3 million was distributed to its shareholders as dividend payments as a result of the company's strong financial position (Lee, 2001). INTRACO's gross cash balances had grown to about S$90 million in October, an increase from S$44 million at the end of June 2001. This was seen to be in excess of its medium-term needs, and some analysts were critical of the payout as it showed a lack of ideas to invest the excess cash to develop and expand the company.

Chapter 7 will raise key factors for the inability of INTRACO to establish itself as a GLC and its eventual takeover by PSC Corporation.

CHAPTER 7

DEVOLVING A GOVERNMENT-LINKED COMPANY — 2000 TO 2003

IS TRADING A NON-CORE FUNCTION?

The new millennium saw the continued strategy of divesting non-core assets and businesses by Temasek Holdings. However, there is reason to pause and reflect whether trading is a non-core function of a state, given that food security and the supply of raw materials continue to be a prime concern of all states and arguably more so for Singapore. A state without any natural resources and lacking an agrarian sector could be left exposed and vulnerable to the fluctuations of global food and commodity prices. It will also pose the argument that the government was willing to divest INTRACO because it already had plans to lure a more established global trading firm to relocate its base to Singapore and invest significant stakes in the firm.

Critics pointed out that INTRACO raked up several business losses and lost its focus because of its divestment of non-core assets and enhancement of its core assets. This had led stakeholders to question the company's strategic value, which by then was to ostensibly overcome the challenge of being redundant and to keep itself relevant through value-added products and services. For example, the INTRACO Enterprise Hub (IEH) was designed to assist local small and medium enterprises (SMEs) to expand overseas.

Some of the questions to be examined include: Did INTRACO outlive its usefulness and why was it unable to refocus its business strategy? Did it become too diverse and unwieldy and unable to expand its profit base?

This chapter will examine the sale and divestment of INTRACO as a government-linked company (GLC).

DIVESTMENT TREND

The new millennium had Temasek Holdings scrutinising its 40-odd major companies, for those that had the potential to push ahead and expand in their respective sectors. Which company could be restructured and which should be sold off? At the time, ownership shares in GLCs accounted for about 13% of assets at Temasek Holdings, which wanted to scale down its involvement in the local economy. Instead of diversification into new businesses, the new mantra was "stay within your core competence; get out of non-core businesses" (Tan, 2003). However, if companies were not discerning and followed this trend blindly, they could needlessly divest themselves of potentially lucrative businesses (Tan, 2003). The Monetary Authority of Singapore (MAS), after some months of quiet persuasion, had announced in mid-2000, a three-year deadline for local banks to dispose of their non-core assets (Lee, 2000). This requirement compelled banks to put up for divestment a dozen or so listed entities. Among them were major companies such as United Overseas Land, Overseas Union Enterprises and Fraser & Neave (Lee, 2000).

The Singapore stock market was also dominated by a large number of GLCs. Many of these GLCs had grown powerful but uncompetitive in the protected domestic market, and found the global economy and external markets to be too competitive to undertake business (Lee, 2000). The publicly listed companies in Singapore had grown too dependent on the domestic market that was increasingly being liberalised and penetrated by larger and more experienced foreign competitors. In order to survive and expand, GLCs had to merge, acquire new assets or agree to buyouts. However, banks and the government had been firm to hold on to the status quo. Nonetheless, faced with the increasing challenges of globalisation that forced the banks to focus on their core competences, it seemed logical for the government to give up control of its GLCs (Lee, 2000). In the case of INTRACO in 2001, the company posted a loss of S$45.8 million. In 2002, it managed to engineer a turnaround into profitability and posted a net profit of S$3.9 million.

INTRACO had a change of CEOs in the new decade when Bernard Chen stepped down from the GLC in October 2000 after nine years as its CEO (Tan, 2000). Chen was concurrently the Member of Parliament for West Coast Group Representation Constituency when he was CEO of INTRACO. During his term at INTRACO, the company's automotive division Intra-Motors initially grew and became a lucrative segment of the group's business (Tan, 2000). However, with the demise of the car dealership business later on, Intra-Motors had to undertake retrenchments and went into receivership. By the mid-1990s, INTRACO's fortunes had plunged and cutting off the motor business helped reduce its losses substantially. Moreover, in 1998, one of INTRACO's subsidiaries Teledata (Singapore) was at the centre of an embarrassing mix-up over a mobile phone tender and was banned from vying for government contracts for two years.[1] The incident exposed vulnerabilities in INTRACO's ability to understand and manage new businesses. Chen's departure from INTRACO followed those of other senior executives such as directors Wee Beng Geok and Tay Kim Hock (Tan, 2000).

For a company of its size, its overall performance had been lacklustre. INTRACO reported an operating loss of $1.4 million on a turnover of S$534.4 million in 2000. In the first half of 2000, its revenue rose by 2.3% due largely to the expansion of the food (46%) and commodities (37%) businesses. Revenue from its engineering and semiconductor businesses was lower due to the depressed state of the construction industry and worldwide shortage of semiconductor components. Instead of diversification, INTRACO's new business strategy was to stay within its core competence areas and exit from non-core businesses. Therefore, entry into the motor vehicle industry typified INTRACO's move into a new industry and it represented close to 10 car brands from Lada to Maserati, Holden and Opel (Tan, 2003). Unfortunately, for GLCs like INTRACO, because of the refocusing on core businesses, they could have needlessly divested themselves of lucrative businesses that were not considered a core competence.

[1] This incident is discussed in Chapter 5 of this volume.

Table 7.1. Group Profit and Loss Accounts 1999 to 2002 (S$'000)

	2002	2001	2000	1999
Turnover	340,834	526,346	534,440	521,832
Cost of sales	(314,834)	(489,899)	(489,952)	(472,897)
Gross Profit	26,000	36,447	44,488	48,935
Other revenue	1,572	3,365	5,879	5,362
Distribution Costs	(28,360)	(60,913)	(39,044)	(38,021)
Administrative Costs	(8,750)	(13,806)	(12,110)	(11,286)
Finance Costs	(1,323)	(2,324)	(608)	(1,866)
Operating (loss)/profit	(10,861)	(37,231)	(1,395)	3,124
Investment Income	6,121	2,435	1,848	2,116
Exceptional items	(11,599)	(19,337)	739	8,984
Share of profits less losses of associates	—	1,146	1,016	7,791
Profit after Taxation	(17,043)	(53,737)	4,285	18,471
Minority interests, net of taxes	4,683	7,900	(558)	51
(Loss)/Profit attributable to Intraco members	(12,360)	(45,837)	3,727	18,522
Earnings per share (cents)	(12.53)	(46.48)	3.84	19.19

Source: Intraco Annual Reports 2000 to 2002.

Table 7.1 shows INTRACO's accounts from 1999 to 2002. The company was fully divested by the government in 2003 and was bought over by PSC Corporation.

Some of the concerns raised by the private sector about the role of GLCs in the domestic economy may have accelerated the trend of divestment. Commentators pointed out that the various legislative acts in Singapore enabled ministers whose ministries are in charge of various GLCs to appoint members of their boards of directors, to request and receive information on their various projects and programmes, and to authorise their raising of loans (Thynne, 1988). Another concern was that the majority of government-appointed directors were public servants, which raised the likelihood that some public sector practices would transfer to the GLCs (Anwar and Choon, 2006, p. 70). Former Prime Minister Lee Kuan Yew commented on the role of public servants in GLCs: "We had to put faith in our young officers who had integrity, intellect, energy, drive, application but no record of business acumen.... We made them entrepreneurs to start up successful companies like NOL and SIA" (Lee, 2000, p. 86). The main concern that the former prime minister had was that GLCs would result in subsidised and loss-making corporations, which INTRACO was turning out to be. In this regard, the board of directors at INTRACO set about trying to turn the GLC around towards profitability.

Au Eng Fong, who previously managed his own group of trading companies, took over as INTRACO CEO in April of 2001 as the company faced an increasingly competitive business environment. He initiated a process of rationalisation and cost-cutting measures such as staff retrenchments (Lee, 2001). There were five rounds of staff retrenchments and staff morale plummeted. He resigned in December 2001 after seven months on the job, having completed his task of streamlining and rationalising INTRACO's businesses ("INTRACO names former ABR boss as CEO", 2003). During his short term in office, the company gave a total payout of S$50.3 million to shareholders despite a net interim loss of S$27.2 million, which was mainly due to a fall of S$20 million in provisions in the value of Development Bank of Singapore (DBS) shares that it held (Lee, 2001). By October 2001, INTRACO had amassed cash reserves of around S$90 million because it had disposed of non-core assets such as DBS shares and improved the management of its inventory and credit.

Some INTRACO investors did not rejoice in the cash payout and voiced concern about the group's perceived lack of focus (Tan, 2002). These investors felt that the company was returning cash because it did not know what to do with the S$90 million received mostly from the sale of non-core assets (Tan, 2002). Analysts also said that the cash return did not signal that the company had any acquisitions in mind, but rather that it signalled an effort by the management to make INTRACO more attractive and cheaper as a takeover target (Tan, 2002). Analysts noted that the proposal to halve the par value of the company's shares could be construed as a need to reflect the true value of the company's assets, which were worth less than before.

At the time, Kevin Scully of NetResearch commented that INTRACO "[was] in need of recapitalising to move forward, which could mean a rights issue" (Tan, 2002). It would also make sense for INTRACO, which was 22.86% owned by Temasek Holdings, to privatise its 50.8% share in Teledata. That way, it could also leverage on Teledata, which had promising prospects as the economy grew (Tan, 2002). In the event of its business model losing its shine or earnings stream declining, INTRACO would still have some S$37 million in cash after the payouts, which was a rarity during those difficult times (Tan, 2002). In early 2002, despite a loss of S$45.8 million in 2001, analysts predicted that INTRACO may still be a good stock to buy based on privatisation, takeover or merger play (Tan, 2002).

Vice-president Leong Siew Hay took over as acting CEO in February 2002. Only in late 2002 did INTRACO appoint Teng Theng Dar from ABR Holdings as its new CEO ("INTRACO names former ABR boss as CEO", 2003). Apart from its trading network, Teng had announced that INTRACO would seek to participate in activities to build water treatment plants, food, energy and infrastructure (Kagda, 2003).

As soon as he took the helm at INTRACO, Teng described his frustrations of trying to turn around a company that had fallen from being a government trading arm to being a loss-making entity. He explained that he would like to build INTRACO into a Singapore brand name in the region, assist in establishing Singapore-based regional companies and strengthen SMEs through the company's trading network (Kagda, 2003). INTRACO would also re-establish its presence in countries such as Indonesia where it had to exit during the Asian Financial Crisis in 1997. Teng announced that he would steer the company away from some of its existing activities that included engineering and projects packaging; industrial marketing and distribution; investments in communications; storage and warehousing. He explained that INTRACO needed to overhaul its business strategy to return to profit after two straight years of incurring losses. He had realised that INTRACO had already lost most of the advantage it had leveraged on through its vast networks and government support (Lim, 2003).

Teng said at the time, "I started the process of re-positioning ourselves, walking around and listening to what people are saying. I want to make sure INTRACO is an entrepreneurial organisation and can take ownership of whatever it does" (Koh, 2003). His main challenge would be to keep INTRACO relevant through value-added products and services.

One way would be to establish an Enterprise Hub, a collaborative plan that gives outward-looking SMEs an established distribution network in the region while at the same time ensuring a stream of new products for INTRACO (Lim, 2003). INTRACO's new business model called for leveraging on its key competency, trading, but at the same time working with SMEs that had the potential to expand into the region. Teng had said, "we want to work with promising SMEs, especially those with the potential for regional expansion to promote the Singapore brand name" (Kagda, 2003). SMEs that had the potential to expand might lack the human resources and experience to do so. Under the new business model, INTRACO would front the SMEs' regional expansion and provide the necessary expertise including gap financing. These networks could also include companies not based in Singapore that were keen to tap into INTRACO's regional network. Small companies would receive other benefits from the hub such as coping with increased business volume, economies of scale and use of INTRACO technology (Chow, 2003). In promoting this hub, the company aimed to raise its profile among exporters so that it could broaden the range of products it distributed in countries such as India and China (Chow, 2003).

Teng announced that INTRACO was in discussions with five SMEs on possible tie-ups, including financial adviser Arka Projects, to help project the INTRACO brand back into regional markets (Chow, 2003). He estimated that it would take at least three years for INTRACO to become a solutions trader. Meanwhile, Singapore-listed PSC Corporation announced in December 2003 that it was acquiring a 29.9% stake in INTRACO for S$18.28 million, which would give it effective control of the company. The shares were bought at 62 cents each from NatSteel, DBS Bank and Temasek Holdings ("PSC man takes over chair at INTRACO", 2003). Allan Yap, who managed Hong Kong-listed Hanny Holdings and PSC Corporation, was named the new chairman of INTRACO, now no longer a GLC. Yap took over as non-executive chairman of INTRACO from NatSteel veteran Ang Kong Hua. Yap was also the executive chairman of PSC which was 27.4% owned by Hanny Holdings at the time ("PSC man takes over chair at INTRACO", 2003).

Figure 7.1 shows the turnover rate for INTRACO versus per share data earnings after taxation from 1990 until its total divestment as a GLC in 2003.

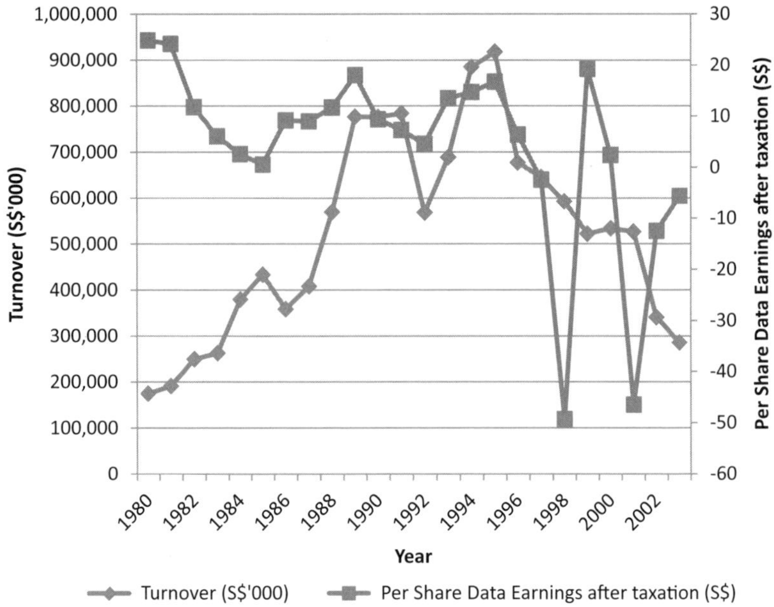

Figure 7.1. Turnover Rate of INTRACO versus per Share Data Earnings after Taxation.

The per share earnings started from a high in 1980 and progressively declined until 1986 when it became the target of a takeover bid by UIC. The share price recovered and was on an upward trend until 1990, just after the Cold War. The trend declined again until 1994 when it recovered before steeply declining until 1998. This was during the Asian Financial Crisis and when INTRACO faced slowing profits and huge losses in the automotive dealership industry. The per share earnings recovered steeply to reach a peak in 1999, and thereafter plunged again to reach a low in 2001 before recovering. The per share earnings were on an upward trajectory until INTRACO's total divestment as a GLC to PSC Corporation in 2003.

Figure 7.2 shows INTRACO's total turnover against turnover for its Singapore operations from 1990 until its total divestment as a GLC in 2003. The general trend showed that INTRACO's total turnover was closely tied to its Singapore businesses with the exception of a two-year period between the second half of 1998 and second half of 2001, where there was a slight divergence because there was increased revenue stream

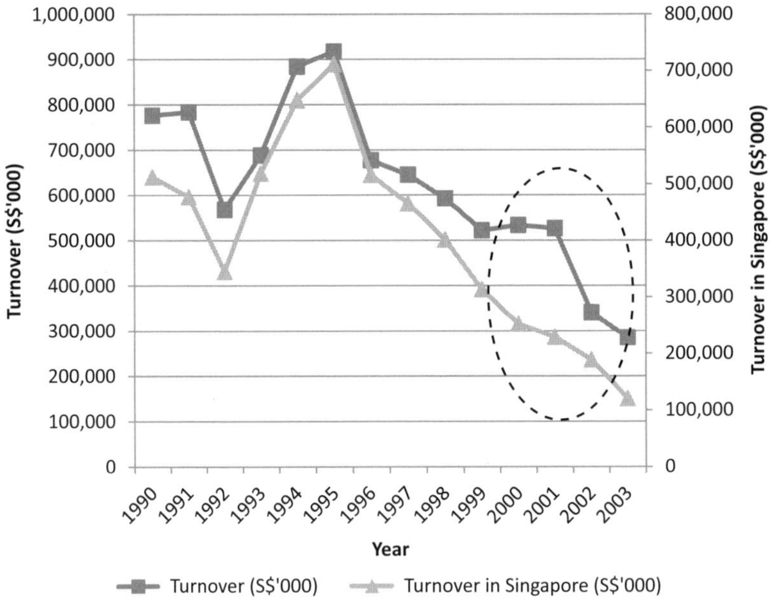

Figure 7.2. INTRACO's Total Turnover against Turnover for its Business in Singapore.

from outside of Singapore.[2] Hence, INTRACO's total turnover was significantly influenced by its Singapore businesses, which indicated that its overseas businesses were of lesser importance than its local operations. Arguably, this indicated that INTRACO did not manage "to blaze its own trail overseas" as it was expected to do in the words of the late Dr Goh Keng Swee, the economic architect behind its inception in 1968. Was there an alternative to INTRACO or a "backup" plan should INTRACO fail?

A GLOBAL SUPPLY CHAIN PERSPECTIVE

Arguably, the formation of INTRACO was to ensure that the formation of global supply chains which spanned multiple stages with each country specialising in a particular good's production sequence did not adversely

[2] See Figure 5.2 of this volume.

impact on Singapore's production capacity.[3] As goods are produced within the framework of vertical specialisation, the establishment of INTRACO by the late Dr Goh Keng Swee was a creation to ensure that Singapore's economy as a node of the vertical specialisation of goods taking place in a fragmented production process across border was viable and sustainable. As shown in Chapter 4 on the need to create a stockpile of rice, INTRACO was used as a key governmental tool to increase Singapore's capacity in terms of food security for a staple commodity.

In terms of Global Supply Chain (GSC) perspective, the importance of raw materials has become critical for all stakeholders in Singapore's economy. In terms of strategic shifts that would impact adversely on specific businesses and cause irreparable harm, the difficulty to acquire raw materials is the most damaging. In this regard, the vagaries and constraints in the supply of raw materials will have an impact on supply chain operations.[4] Three types of outcomes may result from the shortage of raw materials: first, technological, in which supply chain stakeholders may have to redesign their products to use less or substitute materials. Second, geographic, in that the upstream supply chain may need to be reconfigured to tap into new sources. Third, in the operational sense, downstream firms may alter their inventory practices or work to recover alternative materials streams.[5] In this context, INTRACO managed to discover new sources of raw materials such as chemicals needed for Singapore's industries during the Cold War in Eastern Europe. These new sources of chemicals that were purchased in large quantities for Singapore firms potentially gave them an advantage in terms of more competitive pricing for their manufactured products. In the decades following INTRACO's establishment, the production processes of goods across borders have become more entrenched and the General Agreement of Tariffs and Trade (GATT) and its successor the World Trade Organisation (WTO) have become the stewards of transborder economic

[3] Costinot, A. and Vogel, J. (2013). "An elementary theory of global supply chains", *Review of Economic Studies* 80(2013): 109–144.

[4] Alonso, E., Field, F., Gregory, J. and Kirchain, R. (2003). *Material Availability and the Supply Chain: Risks, Effects, and Responses.* United States: MIT.

[5] *Ibid.*

activities.[6] However, this does not detract from the fact that INTRACO itself was a GLC and answerable to its shareholders. Arguably, the shareholder capitalist system that pervades in Singapore would not be as nurturing as a stakeholder type of capitalism that is found say in Japan or Germany. In this regard, the shareholder capitalist system in Singapore in which the state practices found a larger and more established global trading firm, Olam International, which it could leverage on to build its capacity as a node in the GSC network.

OLAM INTERNATIONAL

In 1996, the Trade and Development Board (now IE Singapore International) invited a foreign trading company named Olam International to relocate their entire operations from London to Singapore. Olam was initially established in 1989 by the Kewalgram Chanrai Group as Olam Nigeria Plc. Its aim was to set up non-oil-based export operations out of Nigeria to secure hard currency earnings to meet the foreign exchange requirements of the other companies in the group that were operating in Nigeria. With the success of this venture, Olam then established an independent export operations entity as well as mechanisms for the sourcing and exporting of other agricultural products not related to the group. The group's agribusiness was headquartered in London and exported under the name of Chanrai International Limited. Founded in 1860, the Kewalram Chanrai Group (KC Group) is one of the oldest international companies in Africa and Asia with a long and successful trading history (Olam website).

Between 1993 and 1995, Olam managed to grow its sourcing and logistical capabilities from a single-country operation in Nigeria to a multiple-origin business located among countries in West, then East Africa and eventually in India. This expansion phase of the company had also coincided with the deregulation of the agricultural commodity markets. Olam relocated its entire operations to Singapore and was awarded

[6] Wagner, S. (2009). "International agricultural trade liberalisation and food security: Risks associated with a fully liberalised global marketplace", *Aussenwirtschaft* 64 (Jahrgang, 2009): 139–165.

the Approved International Trader status (now known as Global Trader Programme), under which the company was given a concessionary tax rate of 10%, which was then reduced to 5% in 2004. When it relocated to Singapore, the group's agribusiness was reorganised to be wholly owned by Olam International Limited in Singapore. Olam then set about establishing sourcing and marketing operations in regional countries such as Brazil, China, Indonesia, Papua New Guinea, Thailand and Vietnam, and emerging regions such as Central Asia and the Middle East.

In 2003, Temasek Holdings sold its remaining shares of INTRACO to PSC Holdings Pte Ltd and fully divested itself of the former GLC. In the same year, Temasek Holdings through its wholly owned subsidiary, Seletar Investments, took an initial stake in Olam. Subsequently in 2005, Olam was listed on the Singapore Stock Exchange (SESDAQ). Why Olam? The company's key business is supply chain management of agricultural products and food ingredients. Olam has an international reach with operations in more than 60 countries with over 11,000 customers. The company has a global employee strength of more than 17,000 and in 2010, had discussed a merger with one of its main competitors, the Geneva-based Louis Dreyfuss Commodities, the world's largest cotton and rice trading company. However, merger negotiations were dropped in early 2011 when the two parties could not find an agreement on details of a potential merger.

Since 2011, Olam has become one of the world's top three suppliers of rice, cocoa and coffee and was expanding into sugar milling, urea plants in Africa and dairy farming in Latin America. In the first half of 2011, Temasek had about 12.95% stake in Olam. By November 2012, Temasek had increased its stake to 16% in Olam ("Olam shares rebound as Temasek keeps key stake", 2012). However, on 19 November 2012, Carson Block, the influential founder of Muddy Waters, a US-based stockbroking company, announced to an investment conference in London that he was betting against Olam. Muddy Waters Research then released a 133-page report supporting Block's criticisms of Olam's accounting practices, debt levels and business model ("Olam shares rebound as Temasek keeps key stake", 2012).

Olam fired with a rebuttal of the claims by Muddy Waters and sued the latter for libel, but its share price had fallen by 21%. Several analysts also warned that Olam needed to shore up its weak cash position after piling up debt to finance expansion ("Olam debt fears still linger", 2012).

In response to the Muddy Waters report, Olam undertook a rights issue of bonds plus free detachable warrants to raise up to US$1.2 billion and shareholders would be able to subscribe to 131 bonds and 162 warrants for every 1,000 shares held. Instead of wavering in its support of Olam, as the second largest investor in the company, Temasek shored up its support for Olam by backing the company's complex-bonds-with-warrants issues.

Furthermore, in addition to its own entitlement of 16%, Temasek pledged to take up any bonds that Olam's other shareholders do not buy (Langer and Stanton, 2012). Thereafter, Temasek Holdings raised its stake in Olam to 18% by buying 23.9 million shares in two consecutive days on the open market through its investment vehicle Aranda Investments ("Temasek further increases stake in Olam", 2012). A Temasek spokesperson had said, "We have invested in Olam over several years. In our judgment, the company represents a reasonably attractive investment over the long term and we are pleased to have the opportunity to add to our stake" ("Temasek further increases stake in Olam", 2012). In the event that the rights issue is shunned by all other investors, Temasek's stake could surge to over 28% (Raghuvanshi, 2012). Olam's stock prices rose steadily and by as much as 8% ("Olam debt fears still linger", 2012). In late December 2012, Temasek increased its stake in Olam to 19% from 18% and in so doing boosted its shareholding in the commodities group for the third time in December 2012 ("Temasek raises stake in Olam to 19%", 2012).

In January 2013, Temasek became Olam's top shareholder by subscribing to a S$712.5 million cash call which raised its share to 24% in Olam ("Singapore's Olam to cut spending, debt after investor pressure", Reuters, 25 April 2013). Effectively, Temasek has put its own reputation on the line and wanted a secure foothold in the commodities sector. Ultimately, Olam was urged to reign in its global expansion plans and generate more cash. Olam bowed to investor pressure and said that it would halve its capital spending until 2016 and trim its businesses.

When the Singapore government divested its shares of INTRACO, arguably it already had an alternative conglomerate in its plan to have some degree of influence on global sources, supply chain and marketing of commodities and products. Contrary to Temasek's divestment of INTRACO as a non-strategic or non-core GLC, Temasek has increased its exposure to the global commodities and energy sector. Regional economist at CIMB Bank, Song Seng Wun commented that Temasek was looking at resources with a long-term view. He added, "commodity prices may be wobbling all over the place now, but when the global economy returns to a normal growth path, then demand for resources will surely pick up. So it's cheaper for Temasek to be early" ("Update 2-Olam, under Temasek's gaze, shifts to slower growth path", 2013).

In Olam, the Singapore government had a "ready-made" conglomerate with more extensive business networks globally and a much larger and influential trading company compared to INTRACO. On 14 March 2014, Temasek Holdings launched an offer for all of Olam's shares that it did not already own through its unit — Breedens Investments.[7] Breedens and its concert party owns 54.8% of all Olam's issued share capital and 48.1% of its maximum potential share capital. Olam's value as an agri-commodities firm by Breedens' is placed at SGD 5.33 billion.[8]

At the close of Temasek's buyout offer at 5 p.m. on 23 May 2014, Breedens and concert parties owned, controlled or have agreed to acquire a total of almost 1.96 billion shares, representing about 80.4% of the total issued share capital of Olam and 71.9% of the maximum potential share capital of the company, according to the filing. In addition, Breedens and concert parties also owned, controlled or have agreed to acquire an aggregate of about 360.7 million warrants, representing 90.7% of the total issued warrants of the company.[9] Chapter 8 will summarise the problems that hindered INTRACO from its objective to blaze a trail overseas.

---

[7] Soh, A. (2014). "Temasek's Olam offer fair but not to all". *The Business Times*, 18 April.

[8] Yun, M. and Burgos, J. (2014). "Temasek unit offers to buy Olam in $4.2 billion cash deal". *Bloomberg*, 14 March.

[9] *Temasek, concert parties own 80% of Olam at close of offer*, Channel NewsAsia Website, 23 May 2014. Available at: http://www.channelnewsasia.com/news/business/singapore/temasek-concert-parties/1118934.html#. Accessed 23 May 2014.

CHAPTER 8

CONCLUSION

When it was founded during the Cold War in 1968, INTRACO was given the licence to roam overseas and, in certain respects, INTRACO was ahead of the curve in forging business links overseas, in particular with the socialist economies. Over time — and more rapidly after the end of the Cold War in the late 1980s and with increasing economic integration of the global economy — INTRACO saw its role diminished in terms of its utilitarian value to the state and local companies. When radical strategic planning changes were required, INTRACO was unable to redefine or reinvent its objectives. What were the factors that hindered INTRACO's ability to redefine its objectives? What were the lessons that could be distilled from INTRACO's story about the links between the state and its government-linked companies (GLCs)?

At the start of Singapore's industrial revolution in the 1960s and 1970s, the state needed labour-intensive factories to solve its high rate of unemployment. The high unemployment rate was exacerbated with the withdrawal of British forces east of Suez, when thousands became jobless with the closure of British military bases in Singapore (Lee, 2000, p. 69). The small and medium enterprises (SMEs) were not able to readily absorb the thousands of unemployed individuals because they did not have the resources to expand their activities and develop market share overseas. In this regard, INTRACO was instrumental in expanding the local economy by procuring raw materials in bulk for local SMEs and connecting them to new overseas suppliers and markets (Interview with a former senior INTRACO executive on 28 June 2011). INTRACO had the support of the state to promote exports and procure resources for fledgling local companies. The company acted as buying agent and traded in various products and its prime objective at the time was to locate new markets and assist local companies to penetrate and acquire market share overseas (Interview with a former INTRACO senior executive on 19 July 2011).

INTRACO's key role was to help resolve problems encountered when Singapore companies traded with socialist economies. In this context, government-to-government agreements were required to facilitate trade and socialist economies preferred to undertake business deals with other state-owned enterprises, enabling INTRACO to thrive and operate in this closed markets because of its links to the government (Interview with a former INTRACO senior executive on 28 June 2011). Under the Singapore Inc. framework, INTRACO created a brand image both locally and overseas that it had the government's support in dealing with socialist economies. In overseas markets, INTRACO had an advantage over local companies because of its government links in dealing with other GLCs. However, in the domestic market, INTRACO was seen as a bully by local traders especially after it helped to establish a rice stockpile in Singapore to stabilise the supply and price of rice (Interview with a former INTRACO senior executive on 26 July 2011). Prior to the establishment of the rice stockpile, the price of rice had fluctuated wildly when supply overseas was disrupted because of poor harvests or inclement weather, and because rice traders had created artificial shortages, which had caused much resentment among the buying public that was already subjected to various hardships such as the oil crisis of 1972–1973 (Interview with a former INTRACO senior executive on 23 June 2011).

There were also complaints that INTRACO was "muscling in" on the steel and building materials sector, which provided supplies for the building boom in the construction of HDB flats in the 1970s and 1980s. At the time, apart from steel, INTRACO also supplied ceramic tiles for the construction of HDB flats.

The first managing director of INTRACO, the late Sim Kee Boon, defended the company's actions because it had to survive and trading was a risky business so they had to be opportunistic when there was a chance to make profits. While local traders complained that INTRACO was given preferential treatment, INTRACO senior executives like Sim Kee Boon thought otherwise. From the government's point of view, INTRACO was treated like any other company; in fact, it had to undertake high-risk businesses but earned low profits.

In the 1970s, the company could not undertake "national service" projects anymore to help further the state's interests but had to increase its own profit margins because it was accountable to its shareholders when it became publicly listed in 1972 (Interview with a former INTRACO senior executive on 7 June 2011). In this regard, it is understandable that INTRACO undertook business in the domestic economy to increase its profits. However, in order for INTRACO to survive, it had to have upstream and downstream linkages with parts of the local economy such as the manufacturing sector, but this faced intense opposition from local traders (Interview with a former INTRACO senior executive on 7 July 2011). Nonetheless, in the 1970s and early 1980s, INTRACO undertook acquisitions of relevant companies and built factories to manufacture goods such as clothing and garments.

INTRACO started as the leading state trading enterprise to facilitate Singapore's economic development, but this role changed in the mid-1980s and arguably it lost its relevance thereafter (Interview with a former INTRACO senior executive on 7 June 2011). While it became increasingly obvious to outsiders that it was not possible for the company to undertake business in the manner like it did during the Cold War, it was also difficult for INTRACO to reinvent itself. Some critics pointed out that the company failed because it did not leverage on its strengths in the early phase of its establishment such as its access to the socialist and emerging economies, to evolve into a proper *sogo shosha*. Furthermore, INTRACO tried to undertake business in all sectors where profit was to be made but where it had no expertise; and some deals went sour because the executives involved did not have the required expertise or knowledge of the sector (Personal interview with a former INTRACO senior executive on 16 June 2011).

A former INTRACO employee explained that INTRACO was ahead of the curve and ventured into several emerging economies to explore business opportunities. INTRACO was effectively the point of a spear in the business sense; however, it had no staff or capacity to follow up in taking advantage of the opportunities that were uncovered. In a risky business sector like trading, there was no follow-through because of a lack of funding to invest in overseas partnerships and a lack of government support (Interview with a former INTRACO senior executive on 12 July 2011).

The bureaucrats involved with INTRACO did not have the appetite for conducting risky business ventures. They pointed out that INTRACO had no macro overview of what they needed to undertake in order to achieve the desired objective (Interview with a former INTRACO senior executive on 12 July 2011). However, this was not entirely the fault of INTRACO because it was grappling with basic fundamentals that threatened the survival of the company, such as the mass exodus of senior executives.

Post-Cold War, the Singapore and global economy had changed significantly with the formation of the initial batch of GLCs such as INTRACO. Without regular reviews of the GLCs' performances by majority stakeholders such as Temasek, there was a tendency for GLCs like INTRACO to drift from their founding goals and obfuscate them with national economic development needs. At the very least, there was a need to evaluate the logic of state involvement in specific markets in order to determine what the objectives of GLCs should be collectively and individually (Forfás, 2010).

In the case of INTRACO, it was often required to implement multiple and at times conflicting objectives. While it was not wrong for GLCs to serve multiple objectives, this would negatively affect their performance if the goals and relative priority among them were left unclear (Forfás, 2010). What could have been done? A single centralised agency that is competently resourced by drawing from existing resources and expertise could be dedicated to GLC supervision, which could improve the state's ability to exercise ownership efficiently and monitor companies under its ownership. There is a need to separate the policy, regulatory and shareholder functions to ensure greater transparency and more conscious decision making where conflicts between goals exist.

During in-depth interviews with former INTRACO senior executives, several common factors surfaced that could help to explain INTRACO's inability to achieve its objective of being a trailblazer overseas for Singapore.

IMPACT OF THE CESS TAX ON LOCAL TRADE RELATIONS

The administration of the CESS tax earned INTRACO the spite and envy of local traders who perceived that the CESS which they had paid to undertake business with the socialist economies was being used by INTRACO to compete with them in the same markets abroad such as China. While local traders were unhappy, they seldom voiced this locally but voiced their criticisms to their counterparts in Hong Kong. The CESS tax of 1/2–1% of the total value of any trade transactions would amount to substantial figures if trade were in the hundreds of thousands or millions in value terms.

The CESS tax that INTRACO had administered under the directive of the Ministry of Finance had created enmity between the company and local traders. The CESS collection also became a problem because it showed up in INTRACO's balance sheets but the company was not allowed to utilise it for their business purposes (Interview with a former INTRACO senior executive on 14 June 2011). In order to reduce enmity with the local traders, INTRACO found innovative ways to utilise the CESS tax collected to benefit the Chinese community such as donating school equipment to Chinese schools and sponsoring the translation of English explanations into Mandarin for educational materials. The CESS account was finally terminated in 1991 after the end of the Cold War and when Singapore established diplomatic relations with China, the remaining funds were used for the establishment of the East Asia Institute.

END OF THE COLD WAR

Some former INTRACO senior executives said that INTRACO had outlived its usefulness because its strategic and political advantage ended with the demise of the Cold War. One former CEO of INTRACO lamented that it was not possible for INTRACO to redefine itself because the global business environment had liberalised a lot over the years (Interview with former INTRACO senior executives on 7 June 2011 and 1 July 2011). INTRACO had missed its golden window of opportunity in the initial years of its establishment to entrench itself in various sectors of the economy. For example, INTRACO could have diversified more into the manufacturing sector because local companies initially found it useful, but this leverage faded and local companies then went directly to the suppliers and buyers and excluded INTRACO as middleman (Interview with former INTRACO senior executive on 16 June 2011).

In the meantime, Singapore companies had evolved and were able to connect to overseas suppliers and markets. In the case of GLCs, they had also become savvier in operating overseas. INTRACO's previous role in connecting local companies to overseas partners especially in emerging economies were already undertaken by IE Singapore (formerly, the Trade and Development Board). In order for Singapore GLCs to invest in overseas markets, the government had to divest their shares in non-core or non-strategic GLCs. INTRACO was not a well-known country brand such as Singapore Airlines or SingTel. Moreover, in certain sectors, its branding was buried or hidden by larger brands such as Epson, Panasonic and AT&T because it undertook contract jobs for these larger and more well-known global companies (Interview with former INTRACO senior executive on 21 June 2011).

"CONTINUAL CHURN" IN HUMAN RESOURCE

Since the start of its establishment, the lack of talent in the trading and marketing sectors hindered INTRACO's expansion as a government trading company. There were not many business executives that had experience being traders (Interview with former INTRACO senior executive on 14 June 2011). The recruitment process was not streamlined and individuals from diverse backgrounds were recruited into the company and placed in types of business where they had no prior expertise. For example, an executive with qualifications and interests in fisheries was placed in the textiles department. INTRACO was not professionally managed in terms of human resource. There was very little in-house training (Interview with former INTRACO senior executive on 26 July 2011). The company had to start from scratch in learning the fundamentals on how to operate as a trading company. For example, bankers had to teach the senior executives at INTRACO, including the late Sim Kee Boon and Ngiam Tong Dow, various business tools such as Freight on Board, Letters of Credit and other such intricacies of trading (Interview with former INTRACO senior executive on 19 July 2011). Arguably, while at the point of its inception, this was to be expected of any newly formed company; over time, however, operational wisdom was not entrenched and institutionalised within the company. For example, there were no company guidelines on trading procedures and often the traders did not have the required knowledge of the products that they are buying and selling (Interviews with former INTRACO senior executive on 28 July 2011 and 16 June 2011).

INTRACO was a good training ground for traders because they were working under challenging environments (Interview with former INTRACO senior executive on 12 July 2011). As the executives had no precedence from which to learn, they had to design their own business models to complete their projects successfully (Interview with former INTRACO senior executive on 14 June 2011). While INTRACO became a training ground for traders, several of the more capable among them left to form their own companies that actually competed for business opportunities with INTRACO (Interview with former INTRACO senior executive on 14 June 2011). The inability to attract good human capital to the company was a perennial problem and some insiders thought it was not a good idea to transform civil servants into traders (Interview with former INTRACO senior executive on 23 August 2011). The company did not provide the motivation and challenges for good traders to remain and as a result, INTRACO acquired a poor reputation and were unable to attract talent. The better performing traders also left INTRACO after short stints with the company because they were able to make more profits independently. Several former INTRACO senior executives said it became obvious that the personnel that were left behind in INTRACO were not of the same calibre as those that had left and the former were not able to further develop INTRACO (Interview with former INTRACO senior executive on 23 August 2011).

Unable to retain talent, INTRACO experienced a continual churn in its human resource. The most damaging blow came in mid-1985, when the company lost its managing director Chandra Das and up to 15 senior executives, with some who went on to join a rival trading company called Haw Par. In the late 1990s, during a phase in restructuring, INTRACO hired a CEO who did not know its business. There were five rounds of retrenchment and the company lost good products such as Ben and Jerry's ice-cream (Interview with former INTRACO senior executive on 28 July 2011). Promising traders and marketers were not keen to join INTRACO because of poor publicity and preferred to join larger and more established companies.

LACK OF KNOWLEDGE AND EXPERTISE

Related to the issue of human capital is the lack of knowledge and expertise in the goods being traded by INTRACO. For example, in the food department, the company had an energetic trader who decided to trade in spice but had no knowledge in the spice trade. The trader bought cardamom from Africa but entrusted the quality of the cardamom to the supplier. When the cardamom arrived in Singapore, the quality had deteriorated and the buyer refused to purchase the shipment. In another trading deal, a company trader had bought copra from the South Pacific islands for local manufacturers in Singapore to make coconut cooking oil. In the 1970s, Singapore had three coconut oil refining plants (Interview with former INTRACO senior executive on 1 July 2011). The trader had no knowledge on how to ship copra. When the shipment of copra arrived in Singapore, most of them had borne shoots and could no longer be used for making oil.

In some cases, such as in timber trading, INTRACO had to find and hire timber experts because it was a large part of their business. When the Indonesian government banned the export of raw timber, INTRACO was not prepared to go into the secondary industry of log processing and timber sawing, and instead sold off their timber concession.

LACK OF FUNDING

The lack of funding was one of the cited reasons that hindered INTRACO's expansion overseas. From 1980 to 1981, there was an effort made to provide the company with stable funding (Interview with former INTRACO senior executive on 7 July 2011). In 1981, the company raised some S$30 million in capital and the shareholder fund was raised to S$94 million to equip the company to undertake larger projects. INTRACO was poised to buy Far Eastern Bank but the Monetary Authority of Singapore (MAS) felt that INTRACO did not have the capacity to manage a bank (Interview with former INTRACO senior executive on 7 July 2011). While the MAS was partly right at the time, it did not look at the potential for INTRACO to have the ability in the near future to manage the bank acquisition (Interview with former INTRACO senior executive on 7 July 2011).

Moreover, since Development Bank of Singapore (DBS) was a major shareholder in INTRACO, DBS could perhaps have undertaken more funding initiatives for the company when the Far Eastern Bank initiative failed to get MAS approval. DBS could have provided the funding for INTRACO to enhance its upstream and downstream linkages with trading and to reduce its vulnerabilities to the global economy. Did DBS have the capacity to assist INTRACO? As a key shareholder, DBS had managed to transfer two of its senior staff to help stabilise and "shore-up" INTRACO after the mass exodus of senior executives in mid-1985 from INTRACO.

Some senior executives felt that INTRACO should have built up its capital base after it was publicly listed, then completely detach itself from the government (Interview with former INTRACO senior executive on 7 July 2011). INTRACO would then be able to buy out the other GLCs and not have bureaucrats on their board of directors. The management would also be answerable only to the shareholders and not to the executive committee consisting of civil servants that were at odds with management. In this respect, one of the senior executives interviewed cited the case of NTUC FairPrice, they were initially allocated at least two shop units in new HDB estates, but they had to sell the goods at a certain price. NTUC senior management made the decision to compete for these shop units and they were freed of government interference in price setting. NTUC could also bid anywhere in Singapore now for shop units.

LEADERSHIP CHALLENGES

The board of directors and executive committee are crucial in any company as they provide guidance for the management in a company. INTRACO's board of directors was made up of representatives whose companies had significant stakes in INTRACO, which included the government. The board of directors could have provided more help with regard to undertaking business with socialist economies or with emerging economies. The directors had appeared to be highly risk-averse and were not keen to support INTRACO in their more risky ventures.

There also appeared to be two conflicting roles for the board at INTRACO: the board had to monitor and check on the activities of the CEO, while also assisting the CEO in facilitating the business transactions of the management. In INTRACO's case, the board of directors seemed only to be interested in the "bottom line" of the company (Interview with former INTRACO senior executive on 7 June 2011). Most of the CEOs at INTRACO were not commodity traders and for INTRACO to be successful, it had to have the profile of a big commodity trader (Interview with former INTRACO senior executive on 12 July 2011). If this had occurred, INTRACO could have entrenched itself into specific sectors like mining, palm oil production or petrochemicals.

Arguably, the company's leaders especially after the mass exodus of senior talent in mid-1986 did not create enough value-added businesses in INTRACO's upstream and downstream activities. Several interviewees felt that in areas such as logistics, INTRACO could have acquired some warehouses and developed a proper supply chain especially in the food sector. For example, in the supply of chicken, INTRACO could have bought some farms, an abattoir, a cold packaging company and some strategic retail outlets. It could have been a significant player in this food sector (Interviews with former INTRACO senior executives on 28 July 2011 and 16 June 2011).

JOINT VENTURE PARTNERS

INTRACO, to a large extent, was dependent on reliable foreign partners in joint ventures. For example, it had a joint venture with Russian company Agrosin whose main business was in fertilisers. The joint venture lasted for 18 years but INTRACO was not in charge because the Russians controlled the supply and buyers. INTRACO's limited role was to provide support for customs clearance, accommodation for travelling company representatives to the region and administrative support (Interview with former INTRACO senior executive on 16 June 2011). However, things changed abruptly when the long-serving Russian managing director left in 2002 and the new managing director did not run the company well and made some poor investments. The Russian partners eventually liquidated the company. INTRACO had been hoping that their Russian partners would help to "open doors" for them in Asia, but were not proactive in pursuing this. Even though they made a profit on selling their 30% share of the joint venture, INTRACO should have increased their share in the joint venture but instead accepted the status quo.

MANAGING GOVERNMENT AND COMPANY LINKS

Apart from the hiring of civil servants as staff in INTRACO, the company also became a holding area for former bureaucrats who were slated for general elections. For example, Ng Pock Too was one such senior executive in INTRACO. INTRACO also had senior executives who were members of parliament, such as Chandra Das and Bernard Chen. This may have created the perception that the company was backed by the government and that it was receiving unfair advantages over its competitors. In fact, INTRACO had to compete like any other private company. The board was made up of individuals from companies that had large stakes in INTRACO itself such as DBS and Natsteel (Interview with former INTRACO senior executive on 8 July 2011). Some senior executives of the company explained that INTRACO's links with the government actually worked against it especially after the Cold War ended (Interviews with former INTRACO senior executive on 7 June 2011 and 26 July 2011).

INTRACO was trading in millions of dollars and had high leverage and senior civil servants on its board of directors; the executive committee often became nervous because they were answerable to the government and shareholders (Interview with former INTRACO senior executive on 12 July 2011). In the trading business, there was a need to maintain presence overseas such as in the representative offices because it showed that INTRACO was committed to their partners and to the business. INTRACO had more than 40 such overseas representative offices in the late 1970s and 1980s, but had to close these because they became very expensive to maintain. It was felt that the state always believed in "parachuting in" when undertaking business ventures overseas, but this did not always work because presence on the ground had to be built to do that (Interview with former INTRACO senior executive on 12 July 2011).

In examining the in-depth interviews with various former senior executives from INTRACO, several factors already mentioned influenced the development of the company. INTRACO did miss its golden window of opportunity at the height of the Cold War in the 1970s and early 1980s, to develop other businesses that would have sustained its growth. The problem of human capital loomed large throughout the company's existence and the mass exodus of senior executives in 1986 including its managing director Chandra Das signalled the slow demise of INTRACO. Das and his team understood that the trading business was not sustainable and were expanding beyond the middleman role by establishing textile factories and food industries among other ventures. However, the state, through the executive committee, was at odds with the management at INTRACO because it was not able to withstand the risks involved in trading. INTRACO did try to build its financial base to have its own sense of autonomy and not be tied to government support, but this failed because of its inability to purchase its own bank. DBS, one of the main shareholders, also did not provide the funding required for INTRACO to diversify into new areas.

The geopolitical environment did INTRACO no favours. The end of the Cold War and normalisation of political relations between Singapore and socialist countries like China removed the non-tariff trade barriers from which INTRACO had previously benefitted. When the international trade regime was recalibrated to move towards liberal trading regimes and greater economic integration, INTRACO's key state objective of dealing with the socialist economies evaporated.

A culmination of factors as mentioned in the Context of Change Model (inner and outer) (Chapter 3) combined to prevent INTRACO from blazing its trail overseas. Could INTRACO have survived and thrived? The continued presence of the Japanese *sogo shosha* speaks volumes. Without an appetite for risks amongst its board of directors and executive committee, a State Trading Enterprise such as INTRACO was doomed to fail. The exodus of INTRACO's management leadership in 1986 further muddied its objective and coupled with a changing global economy, INTRACO could not restructure and redefine its objective(s).

Is trading and control of supply networks in commodities a non-core function? The inability of INTRACO to control the supply of commodities at source and inability to influence demand made INTRACO vulnerable because other "middleman" trading companies could always marginalise INTRACO from business deals. INTRACO was not able to "value add" to the services it performed to suppliers and consumers. In this context, the government appears to have found a commodities trading company with a global network to secure commodities' supply and markets. Through the Trade and Development Board (now IE Singapore), the government invited trading giant Olam International to relocate to

Singapore by offering the foreign conglomerate attractive incentive schemes. Thereafter, Temasek bought substantial shares into Olam when the latter's share price was sliding. When others sold Olam shares, Temasek shored up Olam's reputation by placing its funds and its own reputation on the line for Olam. Temasek became the largest shareholder of Olam with a 24% share of the company. As of March 2013, Olam's net profit for the first quarter on 2013 was $108.5 million as compared to S$98.7 million in the first quarter of 2012, indicating a net profit rise of 10% ("Olam International net proft rises 10%, *Fox News*, 14 May 2013).

The success of the *sogo shoshas* shows that it should have been possible for INTRACO to remain relevant, compete and expand over the years. It failed to do so because of several factors. A changing geopolitical landscape with the ending of the Cold War had effectively eradicated the artificial socialist economies that INTRACO could leverage for businesses. In terms of leadership and governance, there was no clear focus and strategic planning. Moreover, INTRACO's aims and objectives were muddied by its links with the state. This resulted in the company's inability to reinvent or restructure its business model as the global economy transformed around it. It never fully recovered from the mass exodus of senior management in the mid-1980s.The shareholder type of capitalism that the Singapore Inc model subscribes to suggests that INTRACO was eventually replaced with Olam, a more established global trading company with a much larger "global foot print" in the Global Supply Chain networks.

REFERENCES

CHAPTER 1

"$30 mil Jurong project to begin soon." *The Straits Times*, 4 September 1968.

Parliamentary Debates Singapore. (1968). *Annual Budget Statement.* Singapore: Government Publication Bureau

Abeysinghe, T. (2007). "Report on Singapore: Economy". Unpublished report. August. Department of Economics, Faculty of Arts & Social Sciences, National University of Singapore.

Baker, J. (2000). "Crossroads, A Popular History of Malaysia & Singapore". Singapore, Kuala Lumpur: Times Book International

"Bank to boost Industry, it will start with $10 million capital", The Straits Times, 24 November 1966.

Chan, C.B. (2002). "Heart Work, Stories of How EDB Steered The Singapore Economy From 1961 Into The 21st Century", Economic and Development Board, Singapore.

Economic Development Board (1963). Annual Report, Singapore.

Hack, K. (2009). "The Malayan Emergency as counter-insurgency paradigm". Journal of Strategic Studies, 32(3):383-414.

Jurong Town Corporation (1969). Annual Report, Singapore.

Lee K.Y. (2000). "From Third World to First, The Singapore Story: 1965–2000". Singapore Press Holdings, Times Editions.

"Men Named To Push S'pore Industry Bid", *The Straits Times*, 17 August 1961.

"New Board will have $100m for lending", *The Straits Times*, 4 April 1961.

"NTUC backs Govt in emergency measures", *The Straits Times*, 8 April 1968.

Singapore, Economic Development Board Website. Available at http://www.edb.gov.sg/content/edb/en.html.

Temasek Holdings (2014).Temasek Charter. Available at http://www.temasek.com.sg/Documents/userfiles/files/Charter_2002.pdf.

Van E.R. (1995) "Singapore's Development Strategy". In *Singapore A Case Study in Rapid Development*, edited by K. Bercuson , pp. 11–19, Washington D.C.: International Monetary Fund.

CHAPTER 2

Abe, Y. *The Management Concepts of Sogo Shosha — A Historical Perspective.* Mitsui & Co. Ltd.

Agrawal, A. and C.R. Knoeber (2001). "Do some outside directors play a political role?" *Journal of Law and Economics* 44(April): 179–198.

Calder, K.E. (1989). "Elites in an equalizing role, comparative politics: Ex-bureaucrats as coordinators and intermediaries in the Japanese government-business relationship". *Comparative Politics* 21(July): 379–403.

Cho, D. "The Japanese *sogo-shosha* and the Korean *chaebol* group: Mechanism as a source of sustained competitive advantage". Unpublished paper, Seoul National University.

Duckett, J. (2001). "Bureaucrats in business, Chinese-style: The lessons of market reform and state entrepreneurialism in the People's Republic of China". *World Development* 29(January): 23–37.

Ellis, P (2001). "Adaptive strategies of trading companies". *International Business Review* 10: 235–259.

Fan, J., J. Huang, F. Oberholzer-Gee and M. Zhao (2009). "Bureaucrats as managers — Evidence from China". Unpublished paper, University of Alberta, 15 March.

Gerlach, M.L. (1992). *Alliance Capitalism: The Social Organization of Japanese Business.* California: University of California Press.

Larke, R. and K. Davies (2007). "Recent changes in the Japanese wholesale system and the importance of the *sogo shosha*". *The International Review of Retail, Distribution and Consumer Research* 17(4): 377–390.

Li, D. (1998). "Changing incentives of the Chinese bureaucracy". William Davidson Institute, University of Michigan Business School, *Working Paper* no. 130.

Miwa, Y. and J.M. Ramseyer (2005). "Who appoints them, what do they do? Evidence on outside directors from Japan". *Journal of Economics & Management Strategy* 14(Summer): 299–337.

Raj, M. and T. Yamada (2009). "Business and government nexus: Retired bureaucrats in corporate boardrooms". *JEL*, 15 January.

Schuler, D.A., K. Rehbein and R.D. Cramer (2002). "Pursuing strategic advantage through political means: A multivariate approach". *Academy of Management Journal* 45Ú 659–672.

Shome, A. (2009). "Singapore's state-guided entrepreneurship: A model for transitional economies?" *New Zealand Journal of Asian Studies* 11(June): 318–336.

Shome, T. (2006). "State-guided entrepreneurship: A case study". *Department of Management and International Business Research Working Paper Series* 4, Massey University.

Tanaka, A. (2008). "Why were *sogo shosha* needed?" *Oikonomika* 44: 171–194.

Tanaka, A. (2009). "The role of *sogo shosha* in mass procurement system of resource: Japan's develop-and-import scheme of iron ore in the 1960s". Paper presented at the Asia-Pacific Economic and Business History Conference 2009, Gakushuin University, Tokyo, 19 February.

Torii, A. and T. Nariu (2004). "On the length of wholesale marketing channels in Japan". *The Japanese Economy* 32(Fall): 5–26.

Uesugi, I. and G.M. Yamashiro (2006). "Trading company finance in Japan". *International Journal of Business* 11: 63–80.

CHAPTER 3

Abeysinghe, T. (2007). "Report on Singapore: Economy". Unpublished report, August. Department of Economics, Faculty of Arts & Social Sciences, National University of Singapore.

Anwar, S. and C.Y. Sam (2006). "Singaporean style public sector corporate governance: Can private sector corporations emulate public sector practices?" *New Zealand Journal of Asian Studies* 8(1): 41–68.

Appold, S. (2002). "Consultation and control: The Singaporean business elite between democracy and authoritarianism". Paper presented at the 2002 Annual Meetings of the American Sociological Association, Chicago, pp. 16–19.

"Diversification from INTRACO". *The Business Times*, 23 October 1979, p. 6.

Falvo, F. and M. Parshad (2005). "The internationalisation process of a firm: The case of Volvo company". Master's thesis, Roskilde University.

Forfás (2010). *The role of state owned enterprises: Providing infrastructure and supporting economic recovery*. www.forfas.ie/media/forfas20100730_Role_of_SOES.pdf. Accessed 16 October 2014.

Heracleous, L. (1999). "Privatisation: Global trends and implications of the Singapore experience". *The International Journal of Public Sector Management* 12(5): 432–444.

Ho, C. (2010). "Sustainable state-owned enterprises: Why governance matters". Speech at the Khazanah Megatrends Forum, 4 October.

INTRACO Limited (2004). "Divestment of interest in subsidiary". Announcement, 19 May.

"Is it time to sell Singapore's prized assets?" *The Straits Times*, 29 April 2000.

Johnston, D.M. (2001). "Public policy challenges and opportunities: An editorial introduction." In *Singapore Inc.*, edited by Linda Low and Douglas M. Johnston. Singapore: Eastern Universities Press.

Lee, K.Y. (2002). "An entrepreneurial culture in Singapore". Address at the Ho Rih Hwa Leadership in Asia Public Lecture, Singapore Management University, 5 February.

Lim, M.H. and K.F. Teoh (1986). "Singapore corporations go transnational". *Journal of Southeast Asian Studies* 17(September): 336–365.

Ministry of Finance (2002). *Government-linked companies.* Budget Speech 2002. Available at: app.mof.gov.sg/data/download/2002/FY2002_Budget_Speech.pdf. Accessed 16 October 2014.

Natsteel Limited (2003). "*Disposal of interest in INTRACO Ltd.*" www.myintraco.com.sg/corp_news/natsteel.pdf. Accessed 16 October 2014.

Ramirez, C.D. and H.T. Ling (2004). "Singapore Inc. versus the private sector: Are government-linked companies different?" *International Monetary Fund Staff Papers* 51: 512.

Sabhlok, A. (2001). "The evolution of Singapore business: A case study approach". *IPS Working Papers* 10: 21.

Saunders, A. and J. Lim (1990). "Underpricing and the new issue process in Singapore". *Journal of Banking & Finance* 14(2–3): 291–309.

Shome, T. (2006). "State-guided entrepreneurship: A case study". *Department of Management and International Business Research Working Paper Series* 4, Massey University.

Sikorski, D. (1989). "The perspective for privatization in Singapore". *Asian Journal of Public Administration* 11: 74–91.

Singapore Department of Statistics (2001). "Contribution of government-linked companies to gross domestic product". *Occasional Paper on Economic Statistics Series* 52(2001): 1–18.

Tay, S.S.C. (Ed.) (2006). A Mandarin and the Making of Public Policy: Reflections by Ngiam Tong Dow. Singapore: NUS Press.

Temasak Holdings (2014). Temasak Charter. Available at www.temasek.com.sg/Documents/userfiles/files/charter_2002.pdf. Retreived 16 October 2014.

Yahya, F. (2005). "State capitalism and government-linked companies". *Journal of Asia-Pacific Business* 6(2005): 3–31.

Zutshi, R.K. and P.T. Gibbons (1998). "The internationalization process of Singapore government-linked companies: A contextual view". *Asia Pacific Journal of Management* 15: 219–46.

CHAPTER 4

"A bad year for INTRACO". *New Nation*, 25 May 1976.

"A second look at DBS and INTRACO". *The Business Times*, 15 May 1979.

"Directorate of INTRACO Limited. Letter from INTRACO to Secretary of the Stock Exchange", 9 December 1974.

"Diversification from INTRACO". *The Business Times*, 23 October 1979.

Foo, C.P. (1979a). "INTRACO bid to clinch picture tube export". *The Business Times*, 11 October.

Foo, C.P. (1979b). "INTRACO set to sign deal with China company". *The Business Times*, 25 October.

Goh, H.F. (1978). "INTRACO on the move". *The Business Times*, 5 May.

Heracleous, L. (1999). "Privatisation: Global trends and implications of the Singapore experience". *The International Journal of Public Sector Management* 12(5): 432–444.

INTRACO (1973). Annual Report.

INTRACO (1977). Company announcement to Singapore Stock Exchange, 19 May.

"INTRACO brings in Indon timber to relieve shortage". *The Straits Times*, 1 February 1973.

"INTRACO's come a long way". *The Business Times*, 12 June 1979.

"INTRACO hit by profit setback". *The Business Times*, 3 August 1977.

"INTRACO invited to send mission to North Korea". *The Business Times*, 11 March 1978.

"INTRACO makes headway". *The Business Times*, 16 July 1979.

"INTRACO offers 2 m shares for sale". *The Straits Times*, 1 December 1972.

"INTRACO secures $2.4 m orders". *The Straits Times*, 13 October 1979.

"INTRACO secures plywood contract from China". *The Business Times*, 3 January 1980.

"INTRACO seeks new export horizons". *The Business Times*, 2 January 1977.

"INTRACO to Lagos Fair". *The Business Times*, 8 November 1977.

"INTRACO to step up tempo in South America". *The Business Times*, 6 March 1979.

Ooi, K.B. (2011). *Serving a New Nation: Baey Lian Peck's Singapore Story*. Singapore: ISEAS.

Lim, C. (1981). "INTRACO sets its sight on China". *The Business Times*, 8 May.

Lim, R. (1980). "Petrochemicals may be sold through INTRACO". *The Business Times*, 18 July.

Lim, R. and C.P. Foo (1980). "INTRACO prepares for oil business". *The Business Times*, 11 September.

Loh, H.Y. (1986). "INTRACO in joint venture with China resources". *The Business Times*, 10 December.

Luo, Y. and J.J. Tan (1998). "Comparison of multinational and domestic firms in an emerging market: A strategic choice perspective". *Journal of International Management* 4: 21–40.

Mehta, H. and S. Lee (1992). "Cess on Viet goods may be scrapped with trade pact". *The Business Times*, 17 July.

Mohan, B. (1973). "INTRACO plan to beat timber shortage". *New Nation*, 12 April.

Parliamentary Debates Singapore (1968). *Annual Budget Statement*. Singapore: Government Publications Bureau.

"Pointer from INTRACO". *The Business Times*, 23 August 1979.

Quek, P.L. (1979). "INTRACO close to $140 m deal in Sri Lanka". *The Business Times*, 25 December.

Sabnani, M. (1977). "Slow trading conditions hit INTRACO". *The Business Times*, 11 August.

Sabnani, M. (1978). "INTRACO marketing efforts pay off". *The Business Times*, 30 March.

Sabnani, M. (1979). "Improved second half lifts INTRACO's profit". *The Business Times*, 2 April.

"Severe setback for INTRACO". *The Straits Times*, 17 May 1973.

Sikorski, D. (1989). "The perspective for privatisation in Singapore". *Asian Journal of Public Administration* 11(June): 74–91.

"Singapore and China: The sweet taste of co-operation". *The Economist*, 21 January 1984.

Tan, A. (1979). "INTRACO looking to record earnings". *The Business Times*, 24 August.

Tan, S.S. (2007). *Goh Keng Swee: A Portrait.* Singapore: Editions Didier Millet.

Tay, S.S.C. (Ed.) (2006). A Mandarin and the Making of Public Policy: Reflections by Ngiam Tong Dow. Singapore: NUS Press.

Zutshi, R.K. and P.T. Gibbons (1998). "The internationalisation process of Singapore government-linked companies: A contextual view". *Asia Pacific Journal of Management* 15: 215–246.

CHAPTER 5

Anwar, S. and C.Y. Sam (2006). "Singaporean-style public sector corporate governance: Can private sector corporations emulate public sector practices?" *New Zealand Journal of Asian Studies* 8(1) June: 41–68.

"Buoyant associates help shore up INTRACO's earnings". *The Business Times,* 27 August 1986.

Chan, O.C. (1986). "INTRACO's heavy provisions for debts result in loss". *The Business Times,* 28 May.

Chandiramani, R. (1988). "Flow of profit in the pipeline". *Singapore Business,* November.

Cheng, N. (1986a). "More senior INTRACO executives may join exodus". *The Straits Times,* 26 August.

Cheng, N. (1986b). "Temasek will not sell INTRACO stake". *The Straits Times,* 27 August.

Cheok, A. (1986). "UIC launches $127 million takeover bid for INTRACO". *The Business Times,* 31 May.

Chng, G. (1989). "Shell seals deal for petrochem stake". *The Straits Times,* 22 April.

"DBS will help INTRACO look for new business". *The Straits Times,* 23 September 1986.

De Silva, G. (1987). "INTRACO appoints three new directors". *The Straits Times,* 10 April.

"Dennis Lee joins INTRACO's board of directors". *The Business Times,* 7 January 1986.

Foo, C.P. (1986). "The last of INTRACO's pioneering managers tenders his resignation". *The Business Times,* 18 June.

Goh, H.F. (1978). "INTRACO on the move". *The Business Times,* 5 May.

"Going places". *The Business Times,* 28 March 1980.

Helmore, R. (1984). "Diamond mining in Angola". *Mining Magazine,* June.

Hsung, B.H. (1981). "INTRACO, Fujian to sign trade pact". *The Business Times*, 14 April.

Huff, W.G. (1995). "The developmental state, government, and Singapore's economic development since 1960". *World Development* 23(8): 1421–1438.

"INTRACO and UIC steal the limelight". *The Business Times*, 4 June 1986.

"INTRACO beefs up management procedures after last year's fraud incident". *The Business Times*, 5 May 1988.

"INTRACO denies any part in rice resale". *The Straits Times*, 16 June 1980.

"INTRACO explains delay in setting up joint venture with China Resources". *The Business Times*, 17 December 1986.

"INTRACO not worried by bleak reports". *The Business Times*, 22 May 1980.

"INTRACO's outgoing MD confident of company's prospects". *The Business Times*, 11 January 1986.

"INTRACO: Pact will not hit existing importers". *The Straits Times*, 21 January 1981.

"INTRACO poised for bigger role". *The Business Times*, 19 June 1980.

"INTRACO recruits new execs in expansion drive". *The Straits Times*, 23 October 1980.

"INTRACO to set up Saudi office later this year". *The Straits Times*, 19 June 1980.

Jarhom, N. (1986). "Poor results force INTRACO to cut dividend". *The Business Times*, 30 April.

Koh, F. (1985). "Singapore firm plans Maldives tourist resort". *Singapore Monitor*, 21 April.

Larke, R. and K. Davies (2007). "Recent changes in the Japanese wholesale system and the importance of the *sogo shosha*". *International Review of Retail, Distribution and Consumer Research* 17: 377–390.

Lim, C. (1981a). "Funds for INTRACO". *The Business Times*, 24 April.

Lim, C. (1981b). "INTRACO sets its sights on China". *The Business Times*, 8 May.

Lim, C. (1988). "Temasek said to be planning to sell block of INTRACO shares". *The Straits Times*, 29 April.

Lim, S.N. (1989a). "INTRACO coping well with changes". *Singapore Business*, May.

Lim, S.N. (1989b). "INTRACO: Reaching beyond trade". *The Business Times*, 14 June.

Lim, R. (1980). "INTRACO prepares for expansion". *The Business Times*, 22 October.

Loh, H.Y. (1986). "INTRACO in joint venture with China resources". *The Business Times*, 10 December.

McLaughlan, L. (1986). "INTRACO recommends rejection of UIC offer". *The Business Times*, 10 July.

Ministry of Trade and Industry (1987). *Report of the Public Divestment Committee*, 21 February.

"No offer received for INTRACO shares: Temasek". *The Straits Times*, 30 April 1988.

Oh, K.N. (1989). "Singapore firms see potential in China; Executives are unfazed by crackdown on protesters". *Nikkei Weekly*, 5 August.

Ong, C. (1981). "One-for-one rights from INTRACO". *The Business Times*, 7 March.

Ong, C. (1985). "Das to quit INTRACO, more resignations and lay-offs likely". *The Straits Times*, 14 December.

Sabhlok, A. (2001). "The evolution of Singapore business: A case study approach". *IPS Working Papers*, October. Singapore: Institute of Policy Studies.

Saunders, A. and J. Lim (1990). "Underpricing and the new issue process in Singapore". *Journal of Banking and Finance* 14: 291–309.

Sikorski, D. (1989). "The perspective for privatisation in Singapore". *Asian Journal of Public Administration* 11(June): 74–91.

"Singapore and China: The sweet taste of co-operation". *The Economist*, 21 January 1984.

Siow, D. (1989). "INTRACO taps Chinese trade with another joint venture". *The Business Times*, 4 July.

"South-east Asians on the move". *The Economist*, 23 July 1983.

"Takeover bids help boost price of three shares". *The Business Times*, 6 June 1986.

Tan, L.H. (2004). "Singapore Inc. versus private sector: are government-linked companies different?" *International Monetary Fund Staff Papers*, 1 September.

"Top management changes at INTRACO". *The Straits Times*, 28 September 1987.

"Tough tests ahead for INTRACO after management exodus". *The Straits Times*, 3 September 1986.

"UIC chief appointed to board of INTRACO". *The Straits Times*, 7 January 1986.

"UIC will have to do better if it hopes to win INTRACO". *The Business Times*, 30 June 1986.

Yong, P.A. (1990a). "INTRACO reaps the fruits of perestroika". *Singapore Business*, November.

Zutshi, R.K. and P.T. Gibbons (1998). "The internationalization process of Singapore government-linked companies: A contextual view." *Asia Pacific Journal of Management* 15: 219–246.

CHAPTER 6

Balan, A. (1990). "INTRACO sets up treasury division to manage cash". *The Business Times*, 10 May.

"China merchants in yet another joint venture". *The Business Times*, 23 June 1990.

Chia, W. (1989). "INTRACO teams up with meat distributor Leong Moh". *The Business Times*, 3 June.

"Consortium of S'pore firms enters ventures with Cambodia". *The Straits Times*, 6 February 1996.

Cua, G. (1995). "INTRACO picks infrastructure as a core area". *The Business Times*, 10 May.

Divyanathan, R. (1995). "12 S'pore companies eye light rail contracts". *The Business Times*, 13 February.

Hadhi, A. (1990). "INTRACO consolidates oil business under subsidiary". *The Business Times*, 27 June.

"INTRACO and Informatics in Vietnam venture". *The Business Times*, 19 November 1994.

"INTRACO buys Teledata stake". *The Straits Times*, 9 April 1994.

"INTRACO expands food trading business in Russia". *The Business Times*, 22 September 1993.

"INTRACO forms seafood processing venture in Russian Far East". *The Business Times*, 23 December 1994.

"INTRACO GM to join local private company". *The Business Times*, 19 April 1990.

"INTRACO invests $2.5 m to revamp computer system". *The Business Times*, 17 September 1990.

INTRACO Limited. Lum Chang Securities Pte Ltd, 12.

"INTRACO set for a brisk revival". *Asian Finance*, July 1990.

"INTRACO set to expand role as oil trader". *The Straits Times*, 27 June 1990.

"INTRACO to widen base of businesses". *The Straits Times*, 6 November 1993.

"INTRACO's new country approach". *The Straits Times*, 9 May 1992.

"INTRACO–HK joint venture to supply fuel to S. China". *The Straits Times*, 27 April 1990.

Kagda, S. (2003). "INTRACO goes beyond trade in big push into Indonesia, China, India". *The Business Times*, 30 May.

"Keeping cool and comfortable in the driver's seat". *The Straits Times*, 20 March 1994.

Koh, E. (1990). "INTRACO in HK tie-up to boost China link". *The Business Times*, 27 April.

Kwang, M. (1990). "INTRACO–Soviet tie-up to trade in electronic products". *The Straits Times*, 13 January.

Lee, R. (2001). "INTRACO CEO to quit after 7 months in job". *The Straits Times*, 20 December.

Lim, S.N. (1989). "INTRACO coping well with changes". *Singapore Business*, May.

Mehta, H. (1993). "S'pore group plans to invest $ 80 m in Viet power plant". *The Business Times*, 24 February.

"More companies set to move into Vietnam with new trade pact". *The Straits Times*, 25 September 1992.

Mulchand, S. (1990). "INTRACO–Soviet tie-up studies PC production". *The Business Times*, 24 April.

Ng, R. (1994). "Teledata to Tap Links with INTRACO in its Regional Expansion". *The Straits Times*, 23 April.

Phua, K.K. (1992). "S'pore Firms Little Hit by UN Embargo on 2 Yugoslav States". *The Straits Times*, 4 June.

Raj, C. (1998a). "INTRACO's teledata barred from govt contracts". *The Business Times*, 20 November.

Raj, C. (1998b). "TAS disbarment: Teledata protests its innocence". *The Business Times*, 24 November.

Tan, J. (1989). "INTRACO moving in new directions". *The Business Times*, 27 July.

Teh, H.L. (1992). "Govt-linked firms in venture to clinch regional energy projects". *The Business Times*, 8 December.

Teh, H.L. (1999). "INTRACO's top telecom man Tay Kim Hock resigns". *The Business Times*, 3 March.

Wong, W.K. (1999). "S'pore firms' divestments expected to be gradual". *The Business Times*, 21 June.

Yong, P.A. (1990a). "INTRACO reaps the fruits of perestroika". *Singapore Business*, November.

Yong, P.A. (1990b). "INTRACO: Technical comment". *Singapore Business*, November.

CHAPTER 7

Anwar, S. and C.Y. Sam (2006). "Private sector corporate governance and the Singaporean government-linked corporations". *International Public Management Review* 7(2): 70.

Chow, H. (2003). "INTRACO unveils strategy to steer profits: Comeback plan will include efforts to raise its profile among exporters distribute wider range of goods abroad". *The Straits Times*, 3 September.

"INTRACO names former ABR boss as CEO". *The Business Times*, 11 December 2003.

Kagda, S. (2003). "INTRACO goes beyond trade in big push into Indonesia, China, India". *The Business Times*, 30 May.

Koh, J. (2003). "INTRACO strategy is to tap into SMEs". *The Business Times*, 6 December.

Langer, C. and D. Stanton (2012). IFR Asia 776, 8 December. Available at www.ifrasia.com/pubindex/ifr-asia-776-december-8-2012/16622.issue. Accessed 16 October 2014.

Lee, H.S. (2000). "Get ready for wave of mergers and acquisitions". *The Business Times*, 23 June.

Lee, K.Y. (2000). *Memoirs of Lee Kuan Yew: From Third World to First.* Singapore: Times Editions.

Lee, S.S. (2001). "INTRACO to make $50 m payout to shareholders". *The Straits Times*, 27 October.

Lim, K. (2003). "Survival plan for INTRACO, solution story for clients". *The Business Times*, 3 September.

Olam website. "Shareholding structure". Available at: http://olamonline.com. Accessed on 15 March 2013.

"Olam debt fears still linger". Reuters, 5 December 2012.

"Olam shares rebound as Temasek keeps key stake". AFP, 29 November 2012.

"PSC man takes over chair at INTRACO". *The Business Times*, 4 December 2003.

Raghuvanshi, G. (2012). "Temasek continues to throw its might behind Olam". *The Wall Street Journal Blog*, 20 December. Available at: http://blogs.wsj.com/deals/2012/12/20/temasek-continues-to-throw-its-might-behind-olam.

"Singapore's Olam to cut spending, debt after investor pressure", Reuters, 24 April 2013.

Tan, A. (2002). "A merger play in loss-making INTRACO? — Planned capital reduction makes it a cheap, attractive target: observers". *The Business Times*, 8 March.

Tan, C. (2000). "New pastures for INTRACO chief". *The Business Times*, 30 September.

Tan, C. (2003). "Non-core, bad? It's not always the case". *The Straits Times*, 17 October.

"Temasek further increases stake in Olam". Channel NewsAsia, 20 December 2012.

"Temasek raises stake in Olam to 19%". Channel NewsAsia, 28 December 2012.

Thynne, I. (1988). "The administrative state in transition". In *Privatisation: Singapore's Experience in Perspective*, edited by Ian Thynne and Mohamed Ariff, p. 31. Singapore: Longman.

"Update 2-Olam, under Temasek's gaze, shifts to slower growth path", Reuters, 25 April 2013.

CHAPTER 8

Forfás (2010). *The role of state owned enterprises: Providing infrastructure and supporting economic recovery*. Available at: http://www.forfas.ie/publications/2010/title,6603,en.php.

Lee, K.Y. (2000). *Memoirs of Lee Kuan Yew: From Third World to First*. Singapore: Times Editions.

"Olam International net profit rises 10%", FOX News, 14 May 2013.

INDEX